CW00322093

TAKE · THE

E

OUT · OF · EATING

FELICITY · JACKSON

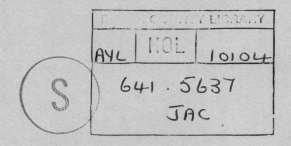

WINDWARD

Editor and contributor: *Felicity Jackson*
Designer: *Caroline Lambourn*
Production: *Richard Churchill*
Additive charts provided by Erik Millstone and
John Abraham.

Published by Windward, an imprint owned by
W. H. Smith & Son Limited
Registered No. 237811 England
Trading as WHS Distributors,
St John's House, East Street, Leicester LE1 6NE

© Marshall Cavendish Limited 1986

ISBN 0-7112-0447-0

Printed and bound in Spain
by Ates Graficas Toledo S.A. D.L. TO: 976/1986

CONTENTS

INTRODUCTION

It has been estimated that three-quarters of the food we eat is processed convenience food, packaged with preservatives, stabilizers, bulking agents, flavourings, colourings and all the other additives which give them a lengthy life on the supermarket shelf. Unfortunately in the process of manufacturing this long-life product, most - if not all - of the nutritional value of the original food is lost.

The additive industry has grown rapidly in recent years to keep pace with the demand for different substances to prevent food going bad, bulk it out with more water and generally hide the effects of the processing, such as loss of colour. The food industry claims that the additives keep the price down; without them the food would have a shorter shelf life, there would be more waste and prices would be higher.

But now with 3,500 additives in use, more and more people are questioning the need for so many additives in our food and concern is growing about the safety of many of them and also about the lack of research into the long-term effects of eating a daily dose of additives.

A processed food rarely contains only one additive, it is usually a mixture of several and the food may then be eaten with another product that also contains a variety of additives. Yet research on additives is usually carried out on animals, testing one additive at a time, not a mixture as happens in real life. No one yet knows what the long-term effects on humans will be. However, certain additives have already been linked with cancer, genetic disorders, hyperactivity and a whole range of other symptoms such as headaches, nausea and skin rashes.

Flavourings and colourings

Flavourings and colourings in particular come in for a great deal of criticism from health experts. Some flavourings are natural but others are cheaper synthetic substitutes which enable the manufacturer to omit the real food altogether. Few consumers realize that there is any difference between the descriptions raspberry flavour, meaning no raspberries — the product merely has to have a similar taste, however it is achieved, raspberry flavoured (meaning there is some real fruit) and raspberry (there is more fruit than in raspberry flavoured).

Because flavourings are not covered by the same regulations as other additives, less is known about what exactly is being added to our food in the way of chemical flavouring than is known about other things like colourings.

Colourings are among the most controversial additives, particularly the yellow colouring tartrazine (E102) which has been linked with serious adverse reactions (see pages 10 and 11 and the charts on pages 116-122). Colourings are purely cosmetic and there is no strong argument for having them in food.

No one knows exactly how much coloured dye we consume per person each year, but one thing is certain a vast proportion of it is eaten by children in the form of highly-coloured foods like packet desserts, soft drinks, sweets, fish products and processed peas. 'Fun' foods such as packet trifle mixes are little more than bulking agents bound together with additives. Children are more vulnerable than adults as their immune systems are undeveloped, and the additives will accumulate in their bodies for longer.

Avoiding additives

It's almost impossible to avoid eating any additives at all; many basic ingredients like margarine contain some. You would need to grow or rear your own food on a plot of land using natural fertilizer to escape them totally. Many are harmless and serve a useful purpose, others certainly prevent fatal cases of food poisoning but there are doubts about their safety.

Avoiding processed foods as much as possible cuts down additive intake to a minimum, and there are plenty of foods that do not contain any additives at all. Fresh fruit and vegetables, fresh meat and fish, milk, eggs and natural yoghurt, nuts, pulses, grains and most dried fruits, wholemeal flour, honey, treacle and molasses are additive-free and can be used to produce all kinds of delicious meals.

This book provides an alternative to convenience food, giving quick, easy recipes for family meals. Each recipe has a box at the end explaining the type of additives that might be found in similar processed versions on the supermarket shelves at the time this book was researched. The charts on pages 116-122 provide a handy reference, so that you can tell at a glance what the additive is and whether it is suspected of being harmful. The fact that a particular additive is used in a product does not mean that a consumer will necessarily suffer the effects mentioned. The charts merely pinpoint the additives which are shown to have links with the various disorders and adverse reactions.

KNOW · YOUR · ADDITIVES

New regulations in 1986 now require all food products sold in Britain to show on the ingredients label any additives that have been used. Vague terms like permitted colouring and preservatives are no longer allowed, though flavourings are not covered by this legislation. The label must state the category of additive and its E number, or if it is an additive used in Britain but not allowed elsewhere in the EEC it must state the category and name.

The EEC Scientific Committee is responsible for drawing up a list of permitted additives that can be used in food that is to be moved from country to country within the EEC. All the member countries have to approve the additives which are then given an E prefix. Some are granted temporary permission for use while research is carried out and these have a number without the E prefix. Individual countries are allowed to use certain additives not approved by the EEC as long as the foods are not exported to countries where the additives are banned. The use of Brown FK in Britain for colouring kippers is an example of this (it is banned everywhere else in the EEC). The additives on the list make up only about 10 per cent of the total number in use as the regulations do not apply to flavourings, enzymes and starches. The E list divides into the following main groups with some miscellaneous additives in each group.

E100-E180 Food Colourings

Some colourings are natural and perfectly harmless, some are synthetic and others are somewhere in between the two. It is the synthetic colourings that cause concern, particularly a group of chemical dyes called azo dyes. They have been linked with many side effects particularly in children and there are strong suspicions that they can cause hyperactivity in susceptible children.

E200-E290 Preservatives

Preservatives are used to stop the natural process of decay by preventing the growth of micro-organisms. Using chemical preservatives is much cheaper than preserving food by drying for instance. Without preservatives there would be many cases of fatal food poisoning from meat products.

However, there is a question mark over the safety of some preservatives, particularly nitrates and nitrites (E249-E252), which are suspected of encouraging cancer in certain circumstances. The food industry argues that the risks of eating nitrates and nitrites are as yet unproven. It would be impossible to produce bacon, ham and many of the other delicatessen-type meats without them, they argue.

E300-E321 Anti-oxidants

Anti-oxidants are added to processed foods to stop their fats and oils going rancid. They are used in many ready-packaged foods and manufacturers claim that it would be impossible to produce many of the convenience foods without them. The most suspect are E320 Butylated hydroxyanisole (BHA) and E321 Butylated hydroxytoluene (BHT). Both are suspected of causing hyperactivity in susceptible people. Adverse reports on BHA included claims that it can raise the level of cholesterol in the blood and interfere with the working of the intestine. Animal studies with BHT have shown liver and kidney damage and abnormalities in offspring. There have been recommendations that BHT should be banned but this has not happened so far, though it is not permitted in foods for

babies and young children except to preserve added vitamin A. BHA is not allowed in food for babies and young children either, except to preserve added vitamin A.

E322-495 Emulsifiers and stabilizers

These are used to bind oil and water together in products such as mayonnaise and prevent them separating into layers. Some are plant gums, some are chemicals and others are synthetically produced derivatives of natural products. Many are safe and natural. Polyphosphates bind water and are used in chicken and delicatessen-type meat products. They enable the food to retain more water during processing so the end product has a higher percentage of water (ie the consumer is paying for water rather than meat). Surveys have found up to 40 per cent water in canned ham.

620-637 Flavour enhancers

Flavour enhancers are used to stimulate the taste buds and make the other ingredients more flavoursome than they really are. They can be added when a product has lost flavour in the processing. The most commonly used one is monosodium glutamate which can have adverse effects such as headaches, dizziness, heart palpitations and nausea.

500-529 Acids and bases

Acids are used to add sharp flavour to foods such as fruit flavoured desserts and fruit based pie fillings. Bases are used to lower acidity in some foods.

530- 578 Anti-caking agents and sequestrants

Anti-caking agents prevent particles of food such as icing sugar sticking together. Sequestrants prevent deterioration of certain foods by inactivating trace metals that would otherwise cause oxidation and make the food rancid.

900-907 Glazing agents

These are substances which are used to give food a shiny appearance or a protective coating. They may be used on chocolates, sweets and chewing gum. Mineral oil, also known as liquid paraffin, is sometimes used on dry fruit.

920-927 Improving and bleaching agents

Bleaching agents are synthetic substances used to bleach flour. They can have adverse effects such as nausea and they destroy much of the vitamin E and nutrients in the flour. Improving agents are used to make bread dough easier to process. They are often synthetic, though vitamin C (E300) may also be used as a flour improver.

SOUPS · PATES · AND · DIPS

Packet and canned soups, bottled dips and bought pâtés of all kinds are among the most convenient of all the processed, ready-to-eat foods and in consequence are all too frequently served up at lunch or snack time. All contain a number of additives and most have Es from every category — colourings, preservatives, anti-oxidants, emulsifiers and stabilizers, yet all are among the easiest of dishes to prepare at home.

Soups

Packet and canned soups are likely to contain some of the following:
Colourings: E102, E110, E122, E123, E124 and E150.
Preservatives: E200, E201, E202, E203, E218 and E220.
Anti-oxidants: E304, E320 and E321.
Emulsifiers and stabilizers: E330, E412, E460.
Flavour enhancers: 621 and 631

Homemade soups need contain none of these and their taste and texture is all the better for it. The all-important basis of a tasty homemade soup is always a well-flavoured homemade stock. Don't use a stock cube unless you are really pushed for time as most chicken and beef stock cubes contain the flavour enhancers 621 and 635 and the colouring E150.

Making a stock is simple: for a chicken stock break up a carcass and place in a large saucepan with some vegetables such as a sliced onion and carrot, 2 or 3 sliced celery stalks, a few pepper-corns, salt and a bay leaf. Add 1.4-1.7 L/2½-3 pints water, bring to the boil, cover and simmer for about 3 hours. Strain and cool. For a beef or lamb stock, ask the butcher for some bones, brown them in a hot oven for 15-20 minutes, strain off any fat and make the stock as above, using the browned bones in place of the chicken carcass. For a vegetable stock, choose a good selection of vegetables — onions, carrots, celery and mushrooms — and brown them in a little oil, then add water, some ripe tomatoes, parsley stalks, peppercorns, salt and a bay leaf and simmer gently for about 1 hour. Stock freezes well or will keep in the refrigerator for 2-3 days.

Pâtés and dips

These are great foods for buffet parties, lunch time snacks or as starters for a more formal dinner. Nothing is easier to make — for many dips the ingredients are simply whizzed up together in a food processor or blender. Pâté ingredients can be quickly mixed up together, cooked, then left to cool. Garnish them just before serving.

Don't undo all the good of making healthy pâtés and dips by serving them with crisps which contain a formidable array of additives. Instead, cut up fresh vegetables, crisp cauliflower, peppers, carrots, cucumber, celery and add button mushrooms, radishes and tiny tomatoes or make potato skins (see Mustard yoghurt dip with potato skins, page 28) which are delicious served hot with a chilled, tangy dip.

Cream of chestnut soup

PEA · SOUP · WITH · CHEESE · TOASTS

Melt the margarine in a large saucepan. Add the onion, potato and peas and fry gently for 5 minutes. Stir in the stock, thyme, lemon juice and salt and pepper. Bring to the boil, then lower the heat and simmer for 20 minutes.

Allow to cool slightly then purée in a blender or food processor until smooth. Return to the rinsed out pan, add the cream and heat gently while preparing the cheese toasts. Do not allow to boil and stir frequently to prevent sticking.

Heat the grill to high, and toast the bread on both sides. Remove from the grill. Mix the cheese with the cream and mustard and season with salt and pepper. Spread the cheese mixture on the toast and heat under the grill until the mixture browns.

Ladle the soup into warmed individual bowls and sprinkle with parsley and cheese. Cut each slice of toast into 4 and serve at once with the soup.

Serves 4

500 g/1 lb frozen peas, thawed
25 g/1 oz margarine or butter
½ small onion, chopped
1 potato, peeled and finely diced
600 ml/1 pint chicken stock
½ tsp dried thyme
1-2 tsps lemon juice
3 tbsps single cream
salt and freshly ground black pepper
1 tbsp finely chopped parsley
25 g/1 oz Cheddar cheese, grated

For the toast:
4 small thick slices wholemeal bread
50 g/2 oz Cheddar cheese, grated
2 tbsps single cream
¼ tsp made English mustard

Make this soup with frozen peas rather than canned ones which may contain flavouring and colourings E102 and E124. Alternatively use soaked dried peas and cook them until tender. This soup is a much healthier alternative to packet pea soups which may contain such additives as preservative E250 if there is ham in the soup; flavour enhancer 621 and anti-oxidant E320.

CREAMY · MUSHROOM · SOUP

Finely chop the mushrooms, reserving 2-3 whole ones for the garnish. Melt half the butter in a frying-pan. Add the chopped mushrooms and fry gently for about 5 minutes until soft. Set aside.

Melt the remaining butter in a large saucepan, sprinkle in flour and stir over low heat for 1-2 minutes until it is straw-coloured. Remove from the heat and gradually stir in milk. Return to the heat and simmer, stirring, until thick.

Remove from the heat, add the cheese a little at a time and stir until melted. Stir in the mushrooms, their juices and the lemon juice. Season to taste. Return to heat and simmer gently for 2-3 minutes.

Pour into 4 warmed soup bowls. Slice the reserved mushrooms and float a few slices on top of each serving. Sprinkle with chives.

Serves 4

250 g/9 oz small button mushrooms
50 g/2 oz butter
2 tbsps plain flour
600 ml/1 pint milk
75 g/3 oz Quark soft cheese
2 tsps lemon juice
salt and freshly ground black pepper
1 tbsp snipped chives, to garnish

Packet mushroom soup may contain flavour enhancer 621; gelling agent E415; anti-oxidants E320, E321. This thick, creamy soup has a delicious flavour without the need for flavour enhancers.

PROVENCAL · FISH · CHOWDER

Heat the oil in a large saucepan, add the onions and garlic and fry gently for 5 minutes until the onions are soft and lightly coloured. Add the tomatoes, with their juice, and the bouquet garni. Bring to the boil, then lower the heat and simmer for 5 minutes, stirring and breaking up the tomatoes.

Add all the remaining ingredients except the fish and the parsley and simmer uncovered, for 15 minutes.

Add the fish to the pan and simmer gently, uncovered, for about 5 minutes, or until the fish is tender but not breaking up. Remove the bouquet garni, stir in the parsley, then taste and adjust seasoning. Serve at once.

Serves 4-6

750 g/1½ lb coley, cod or haddock fillets, skinned and cut into 4 cm/1½ inch pieces
3 tbsps vegetable oil
500 g/1 lb onions, grated
1 garlic clove, crushed
850 g/28 oz can tomatoes
bouquet garni
2 potatoes, cut into 1 cm/½ inch cubes
24 small black olives, halved and stoned
2 tbsps capers, drained
300 ml/½ pint tomato juice
600 ml/1 pint vegetable stock
salt and freshly ground black pepper
3 tbsps finely chopped fresh parsley

> **Use vegetable stock (see page 12) or vegetable cooking water and you have delicious additive-free soup. Similar canned fish soups may contain starch, stabilizers and flavour enhancers 621 and 631.**

OXTAIL · SOUP

Heat the oil in a large saucepan. Add the oxtail pieces and fry over a medium heat until browned all over. Remove and drain on absorbent paper.

Add the flour to the fat in the pan and stir over a medium heat until very brown. Gradually add the stock, whisking constantly, then bring to the boil. Add the onion, carrots, potato, bouquet garni and oxtail. Bring to the boil again, then lower the heat and simmer gently, partially covered, for 2 hours or until the oxtail is tender.

Skim off any scum. Remove the oxtail pieces, cut away the meat and set aside. Discard the bones, fat and gristle.

Purée the soup in batches in a blender or food processor. Return to the rinsed out pan and stir in the tomato purée and reserved meat. Season to taste with salt and pepper and bring back to the boil. Spoon into individual bowls and serve at once.

Serves 8

1 oxtail, cut into pieces
4 tbsps vegetable oil
5 tbsps plain flour
2.3 L/4 pints beef stock (see page 12)
1 onion, chopped
2 carrots, chopped
1 large potato, diced
bouquet garni
1 tbsp tomato purée
salt and freshly ground black pepper

> **Packet oxtail soup may contain flavour enhancers 621, 627 and 631; colouring E150 and preservative E220. Canned oxtail soup usually also contains flavour enhancer 621 and colouring E150.**

KIDNEY · SOUP · WITH · DUMPLINGS

Put the kidneys in a large saucepan with the onion, carrot, chicken stock and tomato purée. Season to taste with salt and pepper, bring to the boil, then cover and cook gently for 15-20 minutes until the kidneys are quite tender.

Make the dumplings: put the sausagemeat, flour, herbs, Worcestershire sauce and egg into a bowl and season with salt and pepper. Using a round-bladed knife, work all the ingredients together to make a slightly sticky mixture. Divide into 12 equal portions. Lift each dumpling on the knife and add to the soup, keeping them separate. Continue cooking the soup for a further 20 minutes.

Using a slotted spoon, lift out the dumplings on to a plate and keep warm while blending soup.

Leave the soup to cool slightly, then work in a blender until smooth. Return to the pan, stir in enough milk to make a runny consistency, then add the dumplings. Heat through for 2-3 minutes.

Transfer the soup and dumplings to 4 warmed soup bowls, sprinkle with parsley and serve at once.

Serves 4

250 g/9 oz lamb kidneys, skinned, cored and finely chopped
75 g/3 oz onion, diced
75 g/3 oz carrot, diced
850 ml/1½ pints chicken stock (see page 12)
½ tsp tomato purée
salt and freshly ground black pepper
about 6 tbsps milk
1-2 tbsps chopped fresh parsley, to garnish

For the dumplings:
100 g/4 oz sausagemeat (see page 33)
2 tbsps plain flour
¼ tsp dried mixed herbs
½ tsp Worcestershire sauce
½ small egg, beaten

> **Use homemade sausagemeat and chicken stock for this recipe. Shop-bought sausagemeat may contain di and tri phosphates; preservative E221; anti-oxidant E300, colouring E127 and emulsifier E412.**

THICK · COUNTRY · SOUP

In a saucepan, heat the oil and butter and gently cook the onion and carrots for 10 minutes.

Add the soup mix together with the chicken stock, leek, celery and herbs. Bring to the boil, then lower the heat, cover and simmer for about 45 minutes.

Season the soup to taste with salt and pepper and stir in the parsley. Serve at once.

Serves 4

1 tbsp vegetable oil
15 g/½ oz butter
1 onion, chopped
225 g/8 oz carrots, sliced
100 g/4 oz packet soup mix (see below)
850 ml/1½ pints chicken stock (see page 12)
1 leek, white part only, chopped
1 celery stalk, chopped
1 tsp dried thyme
1 bay leaf
salt and freshly ground black pepper
1 tbsp chopped fresh parsley

Packets of soup mix are available in most health food shops and some large supermarkets. They usually contain a mixture of lentils, yellow and green split peas, pearl barley and oatmeal. Shop-bought canned thick vegetable soups may contain flavour enhancer 621 and colour E160(a). Packet vegetable soups may contain flavour enhancers 621 and 635; emulsifiers E340, E471 and E472; thickener E415; colouring E102; preservative E220; anti-oxidants E320 and E321 as well as various flavourings.

CREAM · OF · CHESTNUT · SOUP

Nick the chestnuts with a sharp knife, then place in a saucepan and cover with cold water. Bring to the boil and simmer for 10 minutes.

Remove the pan from the heat, then take out the chestnuts, a few at a time. Remove both the outside and inside skins.

Put the peeled chestnuts into a large pan together with the chicken stock, bay leaf and onions. Bring to the boil, then lower the heat, cover and simmer gently for 1½ hours. Remove the bay leaf, then press through a sieve or work in a blender.

Return the soup to the rinsed-out pan and gradually stir in enough milk to make it a smooth consistency. Heat through gently.

Blend the egg yolk and cream in a bowl. Remove the pan from the heat and stir in the egg and cream. Reheat if necessary, but do not boil.

Add the nutmeg, and season to taste with salt and pepper. Add the sugar, a little at a time, to taste. Pour into warmed individual soup bowls and serve at once.

Serves 4-6

750 g/1½ lb fresh chestnuts
1.25 L/2 pints chicken stock (see page 12)
1 bay leaf
2 onions, sliced
about 150 ml/¼ pint milk
1 egg yolk
150 ml/¼ pint whipping cream
pinch of freshly grated nutmeg
salt and freshly ground black pepper
1-2 tsps sugar

This delicious winter soup is completely free of additives if you make your own chicken stock. Chicken stock cubes may contain flavour enhancers 621 and 635; colouring E150 and flavouring.

BROAD · BEAN · AND · CELERY · SOUP

Put the broad beans, celery, stock, thyme and salt and pepper to taste into a large saucepan and bring to the boil, stirring frequently. Skim off any scum with a slotted spoon, reduce the heat to low and simmer very gently for about 1-1½ hours or until both the vegetables are very soft and thoroughly cooked.

Allow the soup to cool a little, then pass it through a sieve or purée it in a blender or food processor. Put back in the rinsed-out pan and adjust the seasoning if necessary.

Reheat the soup gently, then pour into 4-6 warmed individual soup bowls. Garnish with a few small sprigs of watercress. Serve at once, piping hot.

Serves 4-6

1 kg/2 lb broad beans, podded, or
500 g/1 lb frozen beans
4 celery stalks, cleaned and chopped
1.25 L/2 pints chicken stock (see
page 12)
1 tsp chopped fresh thyme or ½ tsp
dried thyme
salt and freshly ground black pepper
watercress sprigs, to garnish

Use homemade stock and you have a wholesome meal with no additives. Packet creamed vegetable soups may include emulsifiers E340, E471, E472; thickener E415; flavour enhancer 621, 635; colouring E102; preservative E220 and anti-oxidants E320 and E321.

TOMATO · RICE · SOUP

Put all the ingredients except the rice, sherry, if using, and parsley into a large saucepan. Bring to the boil, stirring, then lower the heat, cover and simmer for 30 minutes, stirring occasionally.

Pass the contents of the saucepan through a sieve, or leave to cool slightly, then purée in a blender or food processor and sieve to remove the tomato seeds.

Pour the sieved tomato purée back into the rinsed-out pan and bring back to the boil. Stir in the rice, lower the heat, cover and simmer for about 15 minutes or until the rice is tender.

Stir in the sherry, if using, taste and adjust seasoning, then pour into warmed individual soup bowls. Sprinkle with parsley and add a swirl of cream to each of the bowls just before serving.

Serves 4

500 g/1 lb fresh tomatoes, chopped
400 g/14 oz can tomatoes
1 tbsp tomato purée
150 ml/¼ pint water
salt and freshly ground black pepper
50 g/2 oz long-grain rice
2 tbsps medium sherry (optional)
1 tbsp finely chopped parsley, to garnish
cream, to finish

> **Shop-bought tomato soups may contain all or some of the following additives: flavour enhancer 621; acidity regulator E340, emulsifiers E471, E472(b); colouring E124, E110; anti-oxidant E320.**

QUICK · BEEF · AND TOMATO · CONSOMME

Melt the margarine in a large saucepan. Add the shallots and fry gently until softened. Stir in the remaining ingredients and season with salt and pepper to taste. Bring to the boil, then lower the heat and simmer gently for 15 minutes.

Discard the bay leaf. Taste and adjust the seasoning. Serve hot.

Serves 4-6

750 ml/1½ pints beef stock (see page 12)
300 ml/½ pint tomato juice
40 g/1½ oz margarine or butter
3 shallots, very finely chopped
2 tbsps dry sherry
1 tsp caster sugar
1 tbsp finely chopped parsley
1 small bay leaf
salt and freshly ground black pepper

> **Quick beef and tomato soups in packets are likely to contain such additives as flavour enhancer 621; acidity regulator E340; emulsifiers E471 and E472(b); colourings E110 and E124; malic acid; and anti-oxidant E320.**

CHICKEN · LIVER · AND · WALNUT · PATE

Wash and trim the livers, removing any discoloured parts with a sharp knife.

Melt the butter in a saucepan, add the chicken livers, onion, garlic, if using and bay leaves. Simmer gently for 10 minutes, stirring from time to time. Remove from the heat and leave to cool for about 30 minutes.

Heat the oven to 170C/325F/Gas 3.

Remove the bay leaves from the liver mixture and put the mixture through a mincer or chop finely. Stir in the remaining ingredients with salt and pepper to taste. Mix thoroughly.

Transfer the mixture to a foil-lined 850 ml/1½ pt round, rectangular or oval terrine, oven-proof dish or tin.

Place the dish in a roasting tin and pour in enough water to come halfway up the sides of the dish. Bake in the oven for 1½ hours or until firm to the touch. Cover the top with a piece of foil if it begins to brown too quickly. Leave until cold then cover and refrigerate overnight.

Serve straight from the dish, or run a knife around the edge of the dish, then invert a serving plate on top of the dish. Hold the mould and plate firmly together and invert them giving a sharp shake halfway round. Garnish with whole walnuts and bay leaves. Serve with fingers of toast and a mixed salad.

Serves 8

500 g/1 lb chicken livers
100 g/4 oz walnut pieces, chopped
100 g/4 oz butter
1 small onion, finely chopped
1-2 garlic cloves, crushed (optional)
2 bay leaves
2 tbsps dry or medium sherry
1 tbsp brandy
2 large eggs, beaten
pinch of freshly grated nutmeg
salt and freshly ground black pepper
whole walnuts and bay leaves, to garnish

Chicken liver pâté in the supermarkets often contains preservative E250; anti-oxidant E300 as well as modified starch to thicken and firm up the finished pâté.

LENTIL · PATE

Put the lentils in a large pan, pour in 600 ml/1 pint stock, then add onion, tomato purée and dried mixed herbs. Season the soup to taste with salt and freshly ground black pepper.

Bring to the boil, stirring to combine the ingredients together, then lower the heat slightly, cover and simmer for about 30 minutes, stirring frequently, until the lentils have swollen and the stock has been absorbed. The lentils should be given frrequent but quick stirs so that the lid is not off the pan for long, otherwise the steam escapes and the lentils will then take longer to cook. If the lentil mixture begins to dry up and stick to the pan, add the rest of the stock, a little at a time. Remove from the heat and leave to cool for about 30 minutes.

Transfer the lentil mixture to a blender and work until smooth, then add the butter, a piece at a time, and work until it is evenly incorporated.

Taste the pâté and adjust the seasoning if necessary. Spoon the mixture into an 850 ml/1½ pint serving dish, level the surface and leave until cold.

Cover the pâté and refrigerate for at least 2 hours before serving, then garnish with coriander and serve straight from the dish.

Serves 6

Variation: For a vegetarian pâté, use a meat free stock made from water left from cooking vegetables or vegetable stock (see page 12).

The lentils can also be served hot as a delicious accompaniment to roast or grilled meat. Use them after cooking, but without cooling or puréeing.

250 g/9 oz split red lentils
600-850 ml/1-1½ pints chicken stock (see page 12)
1 onion, finely chopped
4 ½ tsps tomato purée
2 tsps dried mixed herbs
salt and freshly ground black pepper
50 g/2 oz butter, diced
coriander sprigs, to garnish

Make your own chicken stock, rather than using a stock cube which may contain the flavour enhancers 621 and 635; colouring E150 and flavouring, and you have a healthy, additive free pâté.

SURPRISE · TERRINE

Heat the oven to 180C/350F/Gas 4.

Wash and trim the livers.

Mince the livers, pork and onion finely in a mincer or chop finely in a food processor. Place in a large bowl and stir in the minced beef, tomato purée, oregano, garlic, if using, and wine. Mix thoroughly and season.

Reserve 3 of the olives for garnish, then halve the rest. Spoon half of the terrine mixture into a 700 ml/1¼ pint deep rectangular dish or tin. Arrange the halved olives sideways in rows across the terrine.

Carefully spoon the remaining terrine mixture on top of the olives and arrange the bay leaves on top. Tap the base of dish a few times. Cover the dish loosely with foil.

Put the dish into a roasting tin, pour in boiling water to come halfway up the sides of the dish and cook in the oven for about 1½ hours. To test for doneness, tilt the dish and if the juices run clear the terrine is cooked. Remove the dish from the roasting tin and cover with foil. Put heavy weights on top, leave to cool, then refrigerate overnight.

To serve: turn the terrine out on to a platter. Slice the reserved olives and arrange them down the centre. Sprinkle a row of parsley either side.

Serves 6

250 g/9 oz chicken livers
250 g/9 oz boneless belly pork, rind removed
1 small onion, cut into chunks
250 g/9 oz minced beef
1 tbsp tomato purée
½ tsp dried oregano
1 garlic clove, crushed (optional)
3 tbsps red wine
salt and freshly ground black pepper
100 g/4 oz stuffed olives
3 bay leaves
1 tbsp chopped parsley, to garnish

Most commercially-produced meat pâtés contain the preservative E250 and may also contain the anti-oxidant E301; emulsifier E471 and modified starch as a thickener to make the pâté firmer. This homemade version does not need any of these additityes.

HERBY · BEAN · PATE

Heat the oven to 200C/400F/Gas 6. Grease an 850 ml/1½ pint soufflé dish, then line base with greaseproof paper and grease the paper.

Melt the margarine in a frying-pan, add the onion and carrots and fry gently for 5 minutes until the onion is soft and lightly coloured. Set the frying-pan aside.

Put the beans in a bowl and mash with a fork, then mix in the eggs. Or, put the beans and eggs in a blender and work until smooth, then transfer to a bowl.

Add the onion and carrots to the beans and stir in the remaining ingredients. Mix well and season with salt and pepper.

Spoon the mixture into the prepared dish and level the surface. Cover with a lid or foil and bake in the oven for 1¼ hours, until just firm all over. Remove from oven and leave to cool for at least 2 hours.

To serve: line a serving plate with lettuce. Run a palette knife around the sides of the pâté and turn out on to the serving plate. Remove the greaseproof paper and garnish with the black olives. Serve, cut into slices, with lightly toasted pitta bread or brown bread and butter, lettuce and cucumber.

Serves 6

Variation: Use two 425 g/15 oz cans red kidney beans instead of the cannellini beans: they will give a reddish-brown coloured pâté. Kidney beans are firmer than cannellini beans and will not mash easily with a fork, so use a blender or food processor to purée them.

2 x 400 g/14 oz cans cannellini beans, well drained
40 g/1½ oz margarine or butter
1 onion, grated
175 g/6 oz carrots, finely grated
2 eggs, lightly beaten
2 tbsps evaporated milk or cream
65 g/2 ½ oz day-old breadcrumbs
3 tbsps finely chopped parsley
1 tbsp finely snipped chives
¼ tsp dried basil
¼ tsp dried thyme
salt and freshly ground black pepper
margarine, for greasing
black olives, stoned, to garnish

> *This pâté makes a tasty snack lunch or supper, and is suitable for vegetarians. Unlike most shop-bought pâté, it has no preservatives or colour and no thickeners or bulking agent to make it look more substantial.*

MIXED · FISH · PATE

Place the tuna and mackerel, with their oil, in a blender or food processor. Pour over the melted butter and add the lemon zest and juice and the garlic.

Blend to a smooth purée. Season well and stir in the cream, if using.

Spoon into individual dishes, cover and chill for 2 hours.

Garnish the pâté with lemon slices and parsley sprigs. Serve chilled, with toast.

Serves 4

Variation: The beauty of this pâté is that it can be made in superquick time from store cupboard ingredients. Other canned fish such as salmon or pilchard can just as easily be used instead of the tuna and mackerel.

175 g/6 oz can tuna fish in oil
125 g/4 ½ oz can mackerel fillets in oil
50 g/2 oz butter, melted and cooled
grated zest of 1 lemon
1 tbsp lemon juice
1 garlic clove, crushed
salt and freshly ground black pepper
1 tbsp single cream (optional)

For the garnish:
few lemon slices
1-2 parsley sprigs

> *Shop-bought fish pâté may contain modified starch as a thickening agent, extra flavouring as well as preservative E223 and colouring such as E171.*

ASPARAGUS · PATE

Drain and discard liquid from can of asparagus and put all but 4 tips into a blender or food processor.

Add the mayonnaise, cream, salt and pepper to taste and blend until purée is quite smooth. If the purée seems to be stringy, sieve it to remove any stringy bits.

Pour the purée into 4 individual ramekin dishes and put into refrigerator for 2-3 hours until firm. Serve chilled, garnished with the parsley and asparagus tips.

Serves 4

275 g/10 oz can asparagus tips
150 g/5 oz lemon mayonnaise
2 tbsps double cream
salt and freshly ground black pepper
parsley sprigs, to garnish

> *A similar bottled dip is likely to contain emulsifiers and stabilizers to prevent the dip separating. Use homemade mayonnaise as commercial ones contain anti-oxidant E320 and flavourings.*

QUICK · PILCHARD · PATE

Drain the pilchards and reserve 1 tbsp of the tomato sauce. Cut the pilchards in half and carefully remove the bones.

Place the fish in a bowl with the reserved tomato sauce, the cream, Worcestershire sauce, Tabasco, lemon juice and gherkins. Beat together thoroughly with a fork and season to taste with salt and pepper.

Spoon the mixture into a serving bowl or 4 individual bowls, cover with cling film and then refrigerate for 30 minutes.

To serve: garnish the pilchard pâté with finely chopped parsley and the prepared gherkin fans and serve chilled with slices of warm pitta bread or oatcakes and butter. As a more substantial snack, serve with a seasonal salad.

Serves 4

Variation: This pâté can also be made with sardines in tomato sauce or with canned mackerel in tomato sauce.

425 g/15 oz can pilchards in tomato sauce
3 tbsps double cream
½ tsp Worcestershire sauce
few drops of Tabasco
2 tsps lemon juice
25 g/1 oz gherkins, finely chopped
salt and freshly ground black pepper

For the garnish:
1 tbsp chopped fresh parsley
4 gherkin fans

A ready-prepared fish pâté may contain additives such as modified starch for thickening, and extra flavourings and colouring E171. It may also contain preservative E223.

TARAMASALATA

Using a sharp knife, carefully peel away the skin from the cod's roe. Alternatively, cut the roe in half and scoop out the inside with a teaspoon.

Put the roe in a blender or food processor. Squeeze the excess water from the bread. Add the soaked bread to the cod's roe.

Work for a few seconds until smooth. With the motor still running, slowly add the olive oil in a thin stream through the hole in the top of the blender goblet, until the mixture is pale pink and creamy.

Add the garlic, lemon juice and the onion, if using. Add pepper to taste and work for 1-2 seconds until thoroughly incorporated. Stir in the natural yoghurt, then transfer the pâté to a serving dish, smooth the surface, then cover with cling film and chill for at least 2-3 hours. Garnish with lemon wedges and black olives and serve with warm pitta bread, cubes of French bread or fingers of toast.

Serves 8

250 g/9 oz smoked cod's roe
100 g/4 oz sliced white bread, crusts removed and soaked in 8 tbsps water
225 ml/8 fl oz olive oil
1 garlic clove, crushed
4 tbsps lemon juice
1 tbsp finely grated onion (optional)
freshly ground black pepper
3 tbsps natural yoghurt
lemon wedges and black olives, to garnish

This taramasalata is paler than a shop-bought one as there is no artificial colouring. Commercial versions usually contain red colouring such as E124 and may also contain preservatives.

COTTAGE · CHEESE · AND YOGHURT · DIP

Sieve or blend the cottage cheese until smooth. Add the yoghurt and mix well.

Wash and trim the spring onions. Chop finely and add to mixture.

Add finely chopped gherkins. Season to taste with salt and pepper and add a few drops of Tabasco sauce, if using.

Give a final mixing. Transfer to a serving bowl and place in centre of a large serving platter. Arrange crudités in groups around the edge of the platter.

Serves 6

225 g/8 oz cottage cheese
2 tbsps natural yoghurt
2 spring onions or ½ onion
4 gherkins, finely chopped
salt and freshly ground black pepper
dash of Tabasco (optional)

Bottled commercial cheese dips may contain anti-oxidant E320; preservative E202 and stabilizer E415. Serve this dip with crudités rather than crisps which contain an assortment of additives, such as colourings E102 and E110; flavour enhancer 621; emulsifiers E322 and E471; and anti-oxidant E320 and E321.

AVOCADO · DIP

Cut the avocados in half lengthways, remove the stones, then scoop out the flesh with a teaspoon. Put the flesh in a bowl and mash it with a wooden spoon.

Add the lemon juice, garlic, if using, and the chopped tomatoes, onion and celery.

Stir in enough olive oil to make a soft, smooth mixture, then add the chopped parsley and season with salt and pepper to taste.

Transfer the dip to a serving bowl, cover with cling film and chill for about 30 minutes. Serve chilled.

Serves 4-6

2 ripe avocados
juice of 1 lemon
1 garlic clove, crushed (optional)
4 tomatoes, skinned, deseeded and finely chopped
1 small onion, finely chopped
4 tbsps finely chopped celery
2-3 tbsps olive oil
1 tbsp chopped fresh parsley
salt and freshly ground black pepper

A similar commercial dip would probably have preservative in it to prevent the avocado spoiling. This dip is quick to make and so delicious that it will be eaten as soon as it is made.

CRAB · DIP · WITH · CRUDITES

Drain the crabmeat and flake it into a bowl. Beat in the yoghurt and chives and season to taste with salt and Tabasco. Refrigerate the dip while preparing the vegetables.

Deseed the pepper and cut into strips about 5 cm/2 inches long and 1 cm/½ inch thick.

Peel the cucumber and cut into sticks the same size as the pepper. Cut the celery and carrots into the same size sticks. Halve the button mushrooms lengthways.

Beat the dip again and spoon into a serving bowl. Put the bowl on a large platter and surround with the prepared vegetables. Alternatively, spoon the dip into a crab shell and arrange the crudités in separate bowls.

Serves 4

175 g/6 oz can crabmeat
150 g/5 oz natural yoghurt
1 tbsp snipped chives
salt
few drops of Tabasco

For the crudites:
1 red pepper
1 cucumber
3 celery stalks
2 carrots
75 g/3 oz button mushrooms

Serve this dip with the colourful crudités shown in the photograph rather than crisps which contain colourings, flavour enhancers, emulsifiers, anti-oxidants and other additives. A similar shop-bought crab pâté may contain preservative and flavouring.

MUSTARD · YOGHURT · DIP · WITH · POTATO · SKINS

First prepare the potato skins. Heat the oven to 200C/400F/Gas 6 and bake the potatoes for about 1 hour until tender. Remove from the oven and raise the heat to 240C/475F/Gas 9. Cut the potatoes in half and scoop out the flesh (use it with another meal). Cut the potato skins lengthways into quarters with scissors, then cut in half. Place on a baking tray and brush all over with melted butter or oil. Season lightly. Bake for 10-15 minutes, turning once, until brown and crisp.

Meanwhile, make the dip. Mix the mayonnaise, yoghurt and mustard together. Spoon into a serving bowl and dust with paprika.

Drain the potato skins on absorbent paper and serve hot with the dip.

Serves 4

6 tbsps mayonnaise
4 tbsps natural yoghurt
4 tsps whole grain mustard
sweet paprika for dusting

For the potato skins:
4 large potatoes
3 tbsps melted butter or oil
salt and freshly ground black pepper

Make your own mayonnaise for this dip. Bought bottled mayonnaise contains anti-oxidant E320 and flavourings. Potato skins are infinitely healthier eating than crisps which are often served with dips.

COURGETTE · DIP

Finely grate the courgettes into a large bowl.

Mix in all the other ingredients, except the olives, adding salt and pepper to taste. Stir until well mixed together.

Transfer the courgette mixture to a serving dish, level the surface, cover and chill for 1-2 hours.

Garnish with the sliced stuffed green olives and serve. Spread on bread or crispbreads for a snack lunch or use as a sandwich filling. Alternatively serve with crudites at the beginning of a meal or with drinks at a party. Arrange the raw vegetables on a serving platter with the courgette dip in a bowl in the centre.

Serves 4

Note: The dip can be kept, covered, in the refrigerator for up to 3-4 days but, because it will harden during this time, it needs to stand at room temperature for about 2 hours before it is served.

250 g/9 oz firm courgettes
100 g/4 oz curd cheese
100 g/4 oz mature Cheddar cheese, grated
50 g/2 oz chopped mixed nuts
2-3 tbsps mayonnaise
2 tbsps lemon juice
1 tbsp ground coriander
salt and freshly ground black pepper
stuffed green olives, sliced, to garnish

This all purpose dip is made from natural ingredients and can be kept for 3-4 days in the refrigerator. The dip is similar to commercial bottled dips and spreads which may contain such additives as anti-oxidant E320; preservative E202 and stabilizer E415.

GINGERED · AUBERGINE · DIP

Heat the oven to 200C/400F/Gas 6. Prick the aubergines all over with a fork, then put them into a roasting tin and bake in the oven for 45-60 minutes, until they feel really soft when they are pressed with the back of a spoon.

Remove the aubergines from the oven and leave until cool enough to handle. Cut them in half lengthways, and squeeze gently in your hand to drain off the bitter juices. Scoop out flesh and leave until cold.

Put the aubergine flesh in a blender or food processor with the yoghurt, the garlic, if using, sugar, ginger, cumin and salt and pepper to taste. Blend until smooth. Transfer to 1 large or 4 small serving dishes. Refrigerate for 2-3 hours to allow dip to firm up.

Just before serving, garnish with coriander or parsley sprigs if liked.

Serves 4

1 kg/2 lb firm aubergines, stems removed
175 ml/6 fl oz natural yoghurt
1 garlic clove, crushed (optional)
1 tbsp light soft brown sugar
1 tsp grated fresh root ginger
½ tsp cumin powder
salt and freshly ground black pepper
fresh coriander or parsley sprigs, to garnish (optional)

Any processed dip containing fresh vegetables like aubergines is likely to have some sort of preservative in it to prolong the shelf life, whereas this dip uses all natural ingredients.

SMOKY · DIP · WITH · VEGETABLES

Purée the tomatoes with the milk in a blender or food processor.

Melt the margarine in a saucepan and sprinkle in the flour. Add the French mustard and chilli powder to taste, and stir over low heat for 1-2 minutes. Remove from the heat and gradually stir in the tomato and milk mixture. Return to the heat and simmer, stirring, until thick.

Add the grated cheese and stir over low heat until the cheese has melted. Put the mixture back into the blender or food processor and work for a few seconds until completely smooth. Season to taste with pepper and transfer to a small serving bowl. Serve the dip warm.

Serves 6

225 g/8 oz can tomatoes, drained
150 ml/¼ pint milk
25 g/1 oz margarine or butter
2 tbsps plain flour
1 tsp French mustard
½-1 tsp chilli powder
100 g/4 oz smoked cheese, grated
freshly ground black pepper

The smoky flavour for this dip comes from the natural ingredients rather than an artificial smoky flavouring. Serve the dip with a selection of crudites such as button mushrooms, carrot strips and cauliflower florets.

CHEESE · AND · HERB · DIP

Put the Wensleydale, Caerphilly or Cheshire cheese into a bowl with the butter, herbs, paprika, caraway seeds and milk. Beat until well blended and creamy, then season to taste with salt and pepper.

Spoon the mixture into a small serving dish, smooth over the surface with the back of a knife and serve with Cheese biscuits (see page 102).

Serves 4

Note: Serve this dip as an unusual starter at a dinner party or, accompanied by vegetable soup, as a quick supper dish.

Alternatively cut out the Cheese biscuits (see page 102) with tiny petits fours cutters, or cut into small straws, and serve at a drinks party. The biscuits may be served slightly warm, if wished.

100 g/4 oz Wensleydale, Caerphilly or white Cheshire cheese, grated
100 g/4 oz unsalted butter, softened
1 tbsp snipped chives
1 tbsp finely chopped fresh fennel leaves or mint
1 tbsp finely chopped fresh parsley
¼ tsp sweet paprika
¼ tsp caraway seeds
4 tbsps milk
salt and freshly ground black pepper

This cheese and herb dip does not have extra additives such as anti-oxidant E320; preservative E202 and stablizer E415 found in some commercial cheese dips.

MEATY · MEALS

Ready-prepared convenience foods have not always been with us and it is not difficult to leave them on the supermarket shelf and make simple meals from natural ingredients.

Beefburgers, sausages and sausage rolls are all popular foods, especially with children, but they are also high in additives when bought ready made, yet they can be made at home very easily with fresh meat which does not contain additives. Homemade sausagemeat is very simple to make (see below) and avoids the di and tri phosphates, preservative E221 and colouring E127 which may be found in manufactured sausagemeat.

Packet meals
Packet meals such as risottos are also high in additives and often contain the suspect colouring caramel (E150). A packet meal such as pork risotto may contain:
Anti-oxidants: E320 and E321
Preservative: E220
Flavour enhancer: 621
Colouring: E150.

Many processed meat products contain the flavour enhancer monosodium glutamate (621) to mask their rather bland flavour -- it is found in everything from sausage rolls and Scotch eggs to canned meatballs and frozen shepherd's pie.

Making the food yourself with fresh good quality ingredients, you can add herbs and spices for extra flavour if you need to.

Canned and delicatessen meats
Canned and delicatessen type meats contain numerous additives including some of the ones causing most concern to health experts. These are the nitrates and nitrites used to preserve many meat products. They are popular with the food manufacturers because as well as being preservatives, they give meats like bacon and ham their attractive pink colour. However, they have been linked with very serious side effects such as encouraging cancer, so they are well worth avoiding whenever possible.

Using fresh meat instead of canned is the best way to avoid nitrates and nitrites and other additives as well. Canned cooked ham, corned beef, chopped pork and pork luncheon meat may contain some or all of the following:
Anti-oxidant: E301
Preservative: E250
Colour: E127
Flavour enhancer: 621
Sodium polyphosphates, Sodium caseinate
Sodium ascorbate
Starch

Moussaka

SAUSAGEMEAT

Mince the pork shoulder and back fat together once or twice, then mix thoroughly with the breadcrumbs if using, season to taste with salt and pepper, then add the spices and sage. If using the breadcrumbs, add a little milk to moisten the mixture slightly, but do not make it sloppy.

Fry a little of the sausagemeat mixture until cooked, then taste it and adjust the seasonings if necessary. Chill the mixture for 10-15 minutes to firm it up, then it is ready to use.

Makes 700 g/1½ lb

500 g/1 lb pork shoulder without rind or bone
225 g/8 oz hard back fat
25 g/1 oz soft white breadcrumbs (optional) plus milk to moisten
salt and freshly ground white pepper
½-1 tsp mixed grated nutmeg, ground mace and ground coriander
¼-½ tsp dried sage

> **Homemade sausagemeat doesn't contain any of the additives found in commercial varieties such as di and tri phosphates; preservative E221; anti-oxidant E300 and colouring E127. Use homemade white bread (see page 95) for the breadcrumbs, if using.**

MOUSSAKA

Put the sliced aubergines in a colander and sprinkle them with salt, turning to coat evenly. Set the colander on a plate and leave to drain for 30 minutes.

Heat about 50 ml/2 fl oz oil in a large, heavy-based frying-pan. Add the onions and garlic and fry over moderate heat, stirring occasionally, for about 15 minutes until golden. Remove from the pan with a slotted spoon, drain on absorbent paper and set aside.

Heat a further 25 ml/1 fl oz oil in the pan. Add the minced lamb and fry gently, stirring often to remove any lumps, for 5-10 minutes until the meat has lost all its pinkness. Remove the mince from the pan and drain on absorbent paper

Rinse the aubergines under cold running water and pat dry with absorbent paper. Heat a further 50 ml/2 fl oz oil in the pan, add the aubergines and fry over moderate heat, turning occasionally, for 10-15 minutes until golden on both sides. Add more oil as necessary. Drain thoroughly.

Meanwhile, put the tomatoes in a saucepan, add the beef stock and basil and season with salt and pepper. Cook over gentle heat, stirring occasionally with a wooden spoon for 10-15 minutes, to make a thick, pulpy sauce.

Heat the oven to 180C/350F/Gas 4. Brush a 30 x 20 x 5 cm/12 x 8 x 2 inch baking dish with oil. In the dish, make layers of aubergines, cheese, minced lamb and onions, seasoning the layers with salt and pepper and moistening with the sauce.

Make the topping: melt the butter in a saucepan, sprinkle in the flour and stir over low heat until straw-coloured. Remove from the heat and gradually stir in the milk. Return to the heat and simmer, stirring, until thickened and smooth. Remove from heat and allow to cool slightly. Beat in the egg yolks and a pinch of nutmeg. Whisk the egg whites until soft peaks form, then fold lightly into the sauce mixture.

Pour the topping over the dish and bake in the oven for about 1 hour, until the topping is browned. Remove from oven and sprinkle with the parsley. Serve hot, straight from the dish.

Serves 6

500 g/1 lb lean minced lamb or beef
1 kg/2 lb aubergines, cut into 1 cm/½ inch slices
salt
about 225 ml/8 fl oz sunflower oil
500 g/1 lb onions, thinly sliced
2 garlic cloves, cut into slivers
750 g/1½ lb tomatoes, skinned and sliced
2 tbsps beef stock (see page 12)
½ tsp dried basil
freshly ground black pepper
250 g/9 oz Gruyère or Cheddar cheese, thinly sliced
2 tbsps chopped parsley:

For the topping:
15 g/½ oz butter
15 g/½ oz plain flour
300 ml/½ pint milk
2 eggs, separated
pinch of freshly grated nutmeg

> **Make your own beef stock and you have all natural ingredients for this recipe. Beef stock cubes may contain flavour enhancer 621 and 623; colouring E150 and flavouring. Convenience meals of ready-made moussaka often contain the colouring E150.**

STEAK · AND · PARSNIP · PIE

Heat the oven to 180C/350F/Gas 4. Heat the oil in a flameproof casserole, add the meat and onion and fry until the onion is soft and the meat is browned on all sides. Sprinkle in the flour, then cook for 1-2 minutes, stirring constantly.

Stir in the tomatoes and their juice. Add the bouquet garni and season to taste with salt and pepper. Bring to the boil, stirring, then cover and transfer to the oven. Cook for 1½ hours or until the meat is just tender. Stir in the parsnips and cook for a further 45 minutes.

Meanwhile, roll out the pastry on a floured surface to a shape slightly larger than the circumference of a 1.1 L/2 pint pie dish. Cut off a long narrow strip of pastry all around the edge. Reserve this and the other trimmings.

Transfer the meat and parsnip mixture to the pie dish, discarding the bouquet garni. Taste and adjust seasoning. Increase the oven temperature to 220C/425F/Gas 7. Brush the rim of the pie dish with water, then press the narrow strip of pastry all around the rim. Brush the strip with a little more water, then place the large piece of pastry on top. Trim the edge of the pastry, then knock up and flute.

Make leaves or other shapes with the pastry trimmings, then place on top of the pie, brushing the underneath with water so that they do not come off during baking. Make a small hole in the centre of the pie, then brush all over pastry with beaten egg.

Bake the pie in the oven for 25-30 minutes until the pastry is well risen and golden brown. Serve hot.

Serves 4

750 g/1½ lb chuck steak, cut into bite-sized pieces
2 tbsps vegetable oil
1 large onion, sliced
25 g/1 oz plain flour
400 g/14 oz can tomatoes
bouquet garni
salt and freshly ground black pepper
250 g/9 oz parsnips, cut into chunky pieces
225 g/8oz puff pastry (see page 75)
a little beaten egg, to glaze

Shop-bought steak pies may contain the colourings E106, E106(a) or (b) and E150, and flavour enhancer 621. Make your own puff pastry (see page 75) or buy ready-made puff pastry without any artificial colourings.

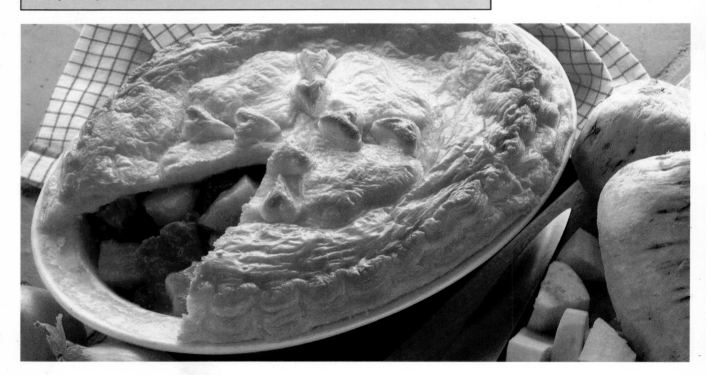

SHEPHERD'S · PIE

Heat the oven to 190C/375F/Gas 5. Heat the oil in a saucepan, add the onion and fry over moderate heat until soft. Add the fresh pepper, if using, and cook for a further 1-2 minutes. Add the meat and cook over brisk heat until browned. Add the mushrooms and canned pimientos, if using, then sprinkle in the flour. Cook for a further few minutes, stirring constantly. Stir in the tomatoes.

Add the tomatoe purée, Worcestershire sauce and oregano to the pan with salt and pepper to taste. Bring to the boil, then lower the heat and simmer gently for 10 minutes, stirring occasionally.

Meanwhile prepare the topping: beat the grated carrot and cheese into the mashed potatoes.

Spoon the mince into an ovenproof dish or 4 individual pie dishes and top with potato. Draw a fork across surface, then bake in oven for 40 minutes.

Serves 4

500 g/1 lb minced beef
1 tbsp vegetable oil
1 large onion, chopped
1 small red pepper, deseeded and chopped, or 175 g/6 oz can pimientos, drained and chopped
100 g/4 oz button mushrooms, halved if large
1 tbsp plain flour
400 g/14 oz can tomatoes, well drained
2 tbsps tomato purée
1 tbsp Worcestershire sauce
½ tsp dried oregano
salt and freshly ground black pepper

For the topping:
1 large carrot, grated
50 g/2 oz Leicester or Double Gloucester cheese, grated
500 g/1 lb potatoes, boiled and mashed with 15 g/½ oz butter and 4 tbsps milk

> **Canned shepherd's pie filling may contain colouring E150; flavour enhancer 621; emulsifier E481 and acidity regulator E450(c). A ready-prepared shepherd's pie often has added colouring E150, and flavour enhancer 621.**

CHICKEN · STIR-FRY

In a bowl, mix together the soy sauce, sherry, ground ginger and cornflour. Stir in the chicken pieces and coat evenly in the mixture. Heat 1 tbsp oil in a frying-pan over moderate heat until very hot, then stir-fry the meat for 1 minute. Transfer the meat to a plate and keep warm in a low oven while stir-frying the vegetables.

Heat the remaining oil, add the vegetables and stir-fry for 1 minute. Add the water and cook for 2-3 minutes. Return the chicken to the pan with the tomatoes. Season and heat through for 1 minute or until hot. Serve the stir-fry at once.

Serves 4

275 g/10 oz boneless chicken cut into bite-sized pieces
2 tbsps soy sauce
1 tbsp sherry
¼ tsp ground ginger
2 tsps cornflour
2 tbsps vegetable oil
3 spring onions
1 small green pepper, deseeded and diced
100 g/4 oz mushrooms, sliced
4 tbsps water
2 tomatoes, sliced
salt

> **A packet dried chicken meal may contain colouring E150; anti-oxidants E320 and E321, preservative E220 and flavour enhancer 621. This quick recipe has no additives.**

MELTING · BEEF · ROLL

Heat the oven to 190C/375F/Gas 5. Put the beef, breadcrumbs, eggs, oregano and garlic, if using, into a bowl. Season and mix thoroughly.

Brush a sheet of foil about 45 cm/18 inches long by 30 cm/12 inches wide with oil. Place beef mixture in the centre and pat into 28 × 20 cm/11 × 8 inch rectangle.

Arrange about three-quarters of the cheese slices on beef, leaving a border of about 2.5 cm/1 inch all round. Starting at 1 short end, roll up the beef like a Swiss roll. Press the join to seal well and press together the ends of the roll to seal in the cheese. Turn the beef so that the join is underneath. Lift the beef, roll on the piece of foil, and place in a roasting tin.

Bake in the oven for about 45 minutes until browned.

Using a fish slice, carefully place the meat on an ovenproof serving dish. Arrange all the remaining cheese slices on top, then return to the oven for a few minutes until the cheese has melted.

Serve at once, cut into slices and garnished with tomato slices.

Serves 4-6

Note: The meat must be finely minced: put it through the mincer twice or grind it in a food processor.

Variation: Dolcelatte or Lymeswold cheese can be used instead of Mozzarella.

750 g/1 ½ lb rump, fillet or good quality chuck steak, finely minced
50 g/2 oz fresh breadcrumbs
2 eggs, beaten
1 tsp dried oregano
1 garlic clove, crushed (optional)
salt and freshly ground black pepper
225 g/8 oz Mozzarella cheese, thinly sliced
vegetable oil, for greasing
tomato slices, to garnish

A similar commercial minced beef roll may contain anti-oxidant; colouring E150 and flavour enhancer 621. Use homemade white or brown bread for the crumbs as shop-bought bread may contain emulsifier E471, E472(e) and E481. Brown bread may contain preservative E280.

STEAK · AND · KIDNEY · PUDDING

Grease a 1.5 L/2 ½ pint pudding basin.

To make the pastry: combine the flour, suet and salt and mix to a soft pliable dough gradually adding the cold water. Cut and reserve one-third of the dough and roll the remainder into a circle until at least 10 cm/4 inches larger all around than the basin. Fold the dough in half, then fold again. Put the dough into the basin, open out and mould to the shape of the basin, folding back any surplus over the rim.

To prepare the kidneys: halve them lengthways, snip out all the white cores and chop.

Season the flour and toss the meat and kidneys in it, then combine with the mushrooms, onion, mustard, herbs and 3 tbsps water. Place in the lined basin. Fold the surplus dough lining down over the filling and brush with cold water.

Half fill a steamer or large saucepan with water and bring to the boil, then lower to a gentle simmer.

Meanwhile, roll out the reserved dough to fit as a lid and place on top of the meat. Seal the edges well and cover them with a lightly greased piece of double thickness foil folded into a pleat. Tie down lightly with string and make a string handle to lift pudding out of steamer. Place in the pan.

Cover the pan with a lid and steam for 4 hours, topping up with more boiling water, if necessary. Garnish with a parsley sprig, if liked.

Serves 4

350 g/12 oz chuck steak, cut into 2 cm/¾ inch cubes
100 g/4 oz ox kidneys, trimmed
25 g/1 oz plain flour
salt and freshly ground black pepper
100 g/4 oz mushrooms, sliced
1 onion, chopped
1 tsp French mustard
¼ tsp dried mixed herbs
margarine, for greasing
parsley sprig, to garnish (optional)

For the pastry:
225 g/8 oz self-raising flour
100 g/4 oz shredded suet
pinch of salt
150 ml/¼ pint cold water

Commercial ready-to-cook steak and kidney puddings often contain the colouring E150 and may also have added flavour enhancer 621, both of which can be omitted in a homemade pudding.

BEEF · AND · LEEK · PATTIES

Bring a saucepan of salted water to the boil. Add the leeks and cook for 12-15 minutes, until just tender.

Meanwhile, put the minced beef in a large bowl and mash well with a wooden spoon to make a smooth paste. Stir in the breadcrumbs, lemon zest and bay leaves.

Drain the leeks thoroughly and chop finely. Drain again on absorbent paper and add to the meat mixture. Season well with salt and pepper and stir in the beaten eggs. Beat well until the mixture is smooth. Cover the bowl with cling film and chill for at least 30 minutes.

Meanwhile, prepare the small leeks for the garnish. Trim the roots and tops from leeks and remove outer leaves. From top of each leek make 8 lengthways slits about 6.5 cm/2 ½ inches long. Plunge the prepared leeks into a bowl of iced water and leave for about 30 minutes until they curl.

Shape the patties: scoop up a heaped tablespoon of the chilled beef mixture.

With floured hands, shape into a patty about 1 cm/ ½ inch thick. Make a further 7 patties in the same way.

Spread the flour out on a plate. Dip the patties into the flour until they are all thoroughly and evenly coated.

Heat the butter and oil in a frying-pan with a lid, add the patties and fry over moderate heat for 4-5 minutes on each side.

Add the lemon juice, cider and water to the pan and season with salt and pepper. Bring to the boil. Lower the heat, cover the pan and simmer very gently for 15 minutes.

Meanwhile, remove the leek frills from the water and pat them dry.

Using a slotted spoon, carefully remove the patties from the pan and arrange them on a warmed serving dish. Pour the sauce over them and garnish the dish with the leek frills. Serve at once while hot.

Serves 4

500 g/1 lb lean minced beef
500 g/1 lb small leeks, tougher outer leaves removed
salt
50 g/2 oz day-old breadcrumbs
finely grated zest of 1 lemon
½ tsp ground bay leaves
freshly ground black pepper
2 small eggs, lightly beaten
plain flour, for coating
25 g/1 oz butter
1 tbsp vegetable oil
juice of 2 lemons
150 ml/¼ pint dry cider
150 ml/¼ pint water
4 small thin leeks, to garnish

These are a healthier alternative to canned meatballs which may contain the flavour enhancers 621 and 631. The patties can be flat as shown in the photograph, or rolled into balls.

SAVOURY · SAUSAGE · CAKE

Heat the oven to 190C/375F/Gas 5. Generously grease a large sandwich tin with margarine.

Sift the flour into a large bowl. Add the remaining ingredients, including the sausagemeat, and season generously with salt and freshly ground black pepper. Knead together well with the hands, until well mixed and of an even consistency throughout.

Press mixture flat in the sandwich tin, and bake in the oven for 40 minutes until the top is golden brown. Leave cake to cool slightly, then turn on to a warmed serving plate and garnish with tomato. Serve cut into wedges.

Makes 8 wedges

500 g/1 lb pork sausagemeat (see page 33)
50 g/2 oz plain flour
4 tbsps milk
1 egg, lightly beaten
1 onion, finely chopped
1 large apple, peeled and roughly diced
1 tbsp tomato purée
½ tsp dried sage
salt and freshly ground black pepper
margarine, for greasing
tomato slices, to garnish

Serve this sausage cake as a snack lunch instead of additive-high sausage rolls. Commercial sausage rolls may contain several or many of the following: acidity regulator E450(c); flavour enhancer 621; colourings E128 and E160(b); anti-oxidants E304 and E307 and preservatives.

SPICED · PORK · SAUSAGES

Crush the peppercorns and juniper berries, making sure that the juniper berries are broken into several small pieces. Add to the minced pork with the herbs and season to taste with salt. Mix well.

With lightly floured hands, form the mixture into 8 sausage shapes. Coat them in the flour seasoned with salt and pepper, dip in beaten egg, then coat again in flour and brush with oil.

Heat the grill to medium. Grill the sausages for 10-15 minutes, turning them several times, until browned on all sides and cooked through. Serve at once, straight from the grill pan.

Serves 4

500 g/1 lb lean pork, minced
12 black peppercorns
4 juniper berries
1 tsp dried mixed herbs
¼ tsp dried sage
salt
65 g/2 ½ oz plain flour
freshly ground black pepper
1 egg, beaten
vegetable oil, to brush

Making your own sausages avoids the possibility of eating the additives di and tri phosphates; emulsifiers E412 and E415; flavour enhancer 621; acidity regulator E338; colouring and preservatives all of which may be found in commercial sausages. The fat content is also much lower in homemade ones.

BEEF · CURRY

Place the beef, onion and garlic in a saucepan and fry over moderate heat until the beef is well browned, stirring constantly to break up lumps.

Stir in the spices and cook for 2 minutes, then stir in the apple, sultanas and the beef stock. Season generously to taste with salt and pepper.

Bring the mixture to the boil, then simmer gently for about 5 minutes.

Stir in the mushrooms and simmer a further 10 minutes. Taste and adjust seasoning. Serve at once.

Serves 4

500 g/1 lb lean minced beef
1 large onion, chopped
1 garlic clove, crushed (optional)
1 tbsp curry powder
¼ tsp ground ginger
¼ tsp ground cumin
1 dessert apple, peeled and grated
2 tbsps sultanas or seedless raisins
300 ml/½ pint beef stock (see page 12)
salt and freshly ground black pepper
100 g/4 oz mushrooms, quartered

No artificial thickeners or colourings are needed in this quick beef curry. Canned beef curry may have added modified starch as a thickener, and colouring E150.

PORK · AND · MUSHROOM · RISOTTO

Melt 40 g/1½ oz of the margarine in a large frying-pan. Add the onions and garlic, if using, and fry gently for 5 minutes until soft and lightly coloured. Add the peppers to the pan and fry, stirring occasionally, for 2 minutes. Remove the vegetables with a slotted spoon and reserve.

Add the cubes of pork to the pan and fry, turning often, for 6-8 minutes until evenly browned on all sides.

Add the rice to the pan and stir to coat all the grains with fat. Stir in the chicken stock. Return the onions and peppers to the pan, add the tomatoes and season with salt and pepper to taste. Bring to the boil, stir well to mix, then lower the heat, cover and simmer very gently for 40 minutes.

Melt the remaining margarine in a small saucepan, add the mushrooms and fry for 1-2 minutes, stirring occasionally.

Stir the mushrooms into the risotto. Taste the rice grains – they should be just tender, but not soft. If necessary, cook for a few minutes longer, adding a little more hot stock if needed. Taste and adjust seasoning if necessary.

Turn the risotto into a warmed serving dish and sprinkle with the parsley and cheese. Serve at once.

Serves 4

350 g/12 oz pork fillet, cut into 2.5 cm/1 inch cubes
50 g/2 oz margarine or butter
2 onions, chopped
1 garlic clove, crushed (optional)
1 green pepper, deseeded and thinly sliced
1 red pepper, deseeded and thinly sliced
300 g/11 oz long-grain rice
about 850 ml/1½ pints hot chicken stock (see page 12)
3 large tomatoes, skinned and chopped
salt and freshly ground black pepper
100 g/4 oz mushrooms, thinly sliced
2 tbsps chopped fresh parsley
50 g/2 oz Parmesan cheese, grated

Packet risotto may contain colouring E150; flavour enhancer 621; preservative E220 and anti-oxidants E320 and E321. Serve this risotto with a salad tossed in oil and lemon juice and French bread with herb butter.

SCOTCH · EGGS

Pat the eggs dry with absorbent paper. Put the sausagemeat into a bowl with the tarragon and salt and pepper to taste. Mix well together.

Divide the mixture into 6 and place on a lightly floured surface. With floured hands, pat out each piece into a circle, about 12 cm/5 inches in diameter.

Sprinkle flour over the surface of the sausagemeat circles and place 1 egg in the middle of each. Gather up the edges of the sausagemeat and bring them around the egg, carefully moulding it to cover the egg completely.

Pour the beaten egg into a shallow bowl and spread the breadcrumbs out on a plate. Wet your hands and roll each egg gently to smooth the surface of the sausagemeat. Dip the Scotch eggs first into the beaten egg, then into the crumbs until well coated.

Heat the fat in a deep-fat frier with a basket to 170C/325F or until a bread cube will brown in 75 seconds.

Very carefully place the eggs in the basket and deep-fry for about 10 minutes until golden brown.

Take the basket out of the oil and lift eggs on to a plate covered with absorbent paper to drain.

Transfer to a clean plate, leave to cool. Serve cold, cut in half.

Serves 4-6

6 eggs, hard-boiled and shelled
500 g/1 lb sausagemeat (see page 33), chilled
2 tsps chopped fresh tarragon or 1 tsp dried tarragon
salt and freshly ground black pepper
plain flour, for sprinkling
1 egg, beaten
50-75 g/2-3 oz fresh breadcrumbs
vegetable oil, for deep-frying.

Commercial Scotch eggs may contain an assortment of colourings such as E102, E124, E128 and E150 as well as flavour enhancer 621. Make your own sausagemeat as shop-bought may contain di and tri phosphates; preservative E221, anti-oxidant E300 and colouring E127.

SAUSAGE · AND · APPLE · TRIANGLES

Heat the oven to 220C/425F/Gas 7. Roll out the pastry on a lightly floured surface to a 35 cm/14 inch square. Cut the pastry into four 18 cm/7 inch squares.

Put the sausagemeat in a bowl and then stir in the apples and onion. Season to taste with salt and pepper.

Divide the sausagemeat mixture between the squares, spreading it diagonally over one half of each of the squares, leaving a 1 cm/½ inch border. Brush the edges of the pastry with beaten egg, then fold pastry over to form a triangle and enclose the filling. Press the edges firmly together to seal them, then knock up with the back of a knife. Brush the tops with beaten egg, then use a sharp knife to make 2 small slits to allow the steam to escape when baking.

Using an egg slice, carefully transfer the triangles to a dampened baking tray. Bake in the oven for 20 minutes, then reduce the heat to 180C/350F/Gas 4 and bake for a further 25 minutes. Cover the pastry with foil during cooking if it shows signs of overbrowning. Serve hot or cold.

Serves 4

350 g/12 oz sausagemeat (see page 33)
2 eating apples, peeled and grated
225 g/8 oz puff pastry (see page 75)
1 small onion, grated
salt and freshly ground black pepper
1 small egg, beaten, to glaze

These make a tastier and healthier alternative to shop-bought sausage rolls which may contain several or many of the following: acidity regulator E450(c); flavour enhancer 621; colourings E128 and E160(b); anti-oxidants E304 and E307 and preservatives.

MUSHROOM · BURGERS

Heat the oven to 190C/375F/Gas 5. Lightly grease a large, shallow ovenproof dish.

Chop the mushroom stalks and put them into a large bowl with the sausagemeat, apple, onion, breadcrumbs and herbs. Mix together well and season to taste with salt and pepper.

Put half the mushrooms into the prepared dish, gill side up. Shape the sausagemeat mixture into 4 burgers and place on each mushroom. Top with the remaining mushrooms and press down gently. Brush a little vegetable oil over the top of each mushroom.

Add the chopped tomatoes, cover with foil and cook in the oven, on the shelf above the centre, for 35-40 minutes until the sausage mixture is cooked. Garnish with parsley sprigs and serve at once.

Serves 4

8 large mushrooms, stalks removed and reserved
350 g/12 oz sausagemeat (see page 33)
1 small cooking apple, peeled and coarsely grated
1 small onion, grated
4 tbsps fresh breadcrumbs
1 tsp dried mixed herbs
salt and freshly ground black pepper
225 g/8 oz can tomatoes, with their juice, chopped
margarine, for greasing
vegetable oil, for brushing
parsley sprigs, to garnish

Make your own sausagemeat for these unusual burgers. Commercial sausagemeat may contain di and tri phosphates; preservative E221; anti-oxidant E300 and colouring E127.

SAUSAGE · PLAIT

Put the sausagemeat into a bowl with the sweet pickle, onion, mustard and herbs. Mix well.

Heat the oven to 200C/400F/Gas 6.

Roll out the pastry on a floured surface to a 30 x 25 cm/12 x 10 inch rectangle. Trim edges, then transfer to a dampened baking sheet.

Mark the rectangle into 3 lengthways and spread the sausagemeat down the central section, in a roll.

Make diagonal cuts 2.5 cm/1 inch apart along the uncovered pastry at each side to within 1 cm/½ inch of the filling. Brush the pastry strips with egg and fold over the sausagemeat to give a plait effect.

Brush all over with beaten egg, sprinkle with poppy seeds, then bake for 45 minutes, or until golden brown. Cover with foil towards end of cooking if overbrowning.

Serves 6-8

750 g/1½ lb sausagemeat (see page 33)
3 tbsps sweet pickle
1 tbsp grated onion
2 tsps made English mustard
1 tsp dried mixed herbs
450 g/1 lb puff pastry (see page 75)
1 egg, beaten
poppy seeds, for sprinkling

Make your own sausagemeat and use either homemade puff pastry, or use commercial fresh puff pastry without artificial colourings.

CHILLI · SAUSAGE · BURGERS

Combine all the ingredients (except the oil) in a large bowl, using floured fingertips to mix well. Season with salt and pepper.

With floured hands, divide the mixture into 4-6 portions and roll them into balls. Flatten each slightly. Chill the burgers for 30 minutes, then leave at room temperature for a few minutes before cooking.

Heat a little oil in a large frying-pan. Fry the burgers for 3-4 minutes on each side or until they are browned and cooked through.

Drain the cooked burgers thoroughly on absorbent paper, then serve at once while very hot. Serve with vegetables or in a soft bun with salad.

Serves 4-6

500 g/1 lb pork sausagemeat
(see page 33)
1 onion, grated
1 large carrot, grated
50 g/2 oz fresh breadcrumbs
4 tbsps tomato purée
1 tbsp chilli seasoning
¼ tsp ground mixed spice
salt and freshly ground black pepper
vegetable oil, for frying

> **Providing you use homemade sausagemeat and homemade bread for the crumbs, these burgers provide a totally additive free meal. Commercial sausagemeat may include di and tri phosphates; preservative E221; anti-oxidant E300 and colouring E127. These burgers are a healthy alternative to ready-made frozen burgers which may contain preservative E225; acidity regulator E450(c); as well as flavour enhancer 621 and flavourings.**

PORK · AND · APPLE · BURGERS

Combine the minced pork, onion, grated apple and sage in a bowl. Season well with salt and pepper. Using a fork, stir in the flour and a little beaten egg to hold the mixture together. Cover with cling film and chill for about 1 hour.

Dip your hands in flour and form the pork and apple mixture into 4 equal-sized round, flat cakes.

Heat the oil in a frying-pan, add the burgers and fry for about 2 minutes on each side. Lower the heat and cook for a further 5 minutes on each side. Transfer the burgers to a warmed serving platter.

Serves 4

350 g/12 oz lean pork, minced
1 onion, finely chopped
1 cooking apple, peeled, cored and grated
2 tsps dried sage
salt and freshly ground black pepper
3 tbsps plain flour
a little beaten egg
2 tbsps vegetable oil

> **This recipe makes high quality burgers with less fat in them than commercial burgers and none of the additives found in burgers such as preservative E223; acidity regulator E450(c); flavour enhancer 621 and flavourings. Packets of pie pork available at supermarkets are perfect for this dish. Alternatively, buy hand and spring of pork from your butcher and ask him to bone it for you.**

MEAT · BALLS · WITH · WALNUTS

Heat the oil in a frying-pan, add the chopped walnuts and fry gently for 5 minutes, stirring often. Remove nuts from the pan with a slotted spoon and drain them well on absorbent paper. Reserve the cooking oil in the pan.

Transfer three-quarters of the nuts to a large bowl. Put the milk in a separate shallow bowl and add the bread. Press the bread down well with a fork to absorb the milk. Break up the soaked bread with the fork and add to the nuts.

Add the minced beef, egg and lemon zest and juice and stir very thoroughly to mix. Season to taste with salt and pepper. Take heaped teaspoons of the mixture and, using floured hands, roll into balls (this quantity should make about 24).

Melt the margarine in a large saucepan, sprinkle in the flour and stir over low heat for 1-2 minutes until straw-coloured. Stir in the stock and simmer, stirring, until thick.

Add the meat balls to the saucepan and bring to the boil. Lower the heat, cover and simmer the meat balls and sauce for 40 minutes.

Stir in the cream and remaining walnuts and heat through gently. Taste and adjust the seasoning if necessary. Transfer to a warmed serving dish, garnish with walnut halves and lemon twists and serve at once with buttered ribbon noodles.

Serves 4-6

Variations: For a spicier sauce, add a pinch of cayenne with the flour.

Walnut oil is expensive but it does give this dish a particularly good flavour. Vegetable oil can be used instead, if wished.

750 g/1½ lb lean minced beef
2 tbsps vegetable or walnut oil
100 g/4 oz shelled walnuts, chopped
125 ml/4 fl oz milk
2 slices wholemeal bread, crusts removed
1 egg, beaten
grated zest and juice of ½ lemon
salt and freshly ground black pepper
15 g/ ½ oz margarine or butter
1 tbsp plain flour
300 ml/½ pint beef stock (see page 12)
2 tbsps double cream

For the garnish:
walnut halves
lemon twists

As well as being healthier, this meat ball recipe has a more delicate flavour than any commercially prepared meat balls. Canned meat balls often contain flavour enhancers 621 and 631, even when they do not have any preservatives, colourings and flavourings.

BEEFBURGER · PIZZAS

Heat the grill to high. Mix the beef and onion and season with salt and pepper. Divide the mixture into 8 and shape each piece into a round, flat patty. Brush with oil and grill for 4-6 minutes, turning them over once during cooking.

Meanwhile, mix together the Cheddar cheese, curd cheese, herbs, and salt and pepper to taste. Put half the mixture into a separate bowl and blend in the tomato purée until well combined.

Leave the grilled beefburgers on the grill rack. Spread half of them with the plain cheese mixture and the others with the tomato-cheese mixture. Arrange 2 anchovy fillets in a cross on each tomato-cheese-topped burger, and 2 pimiento strips in a cross on each plain cheese-topped burger. Garnish the top of each beefburger pizza with 2 black olive halves.

Grill the burgers for 2-3 minutes until the cheese topping is golden. Serve at once, giving each person one of each kind of pizza, for a delicious lunch or supper, with a lettuce, tomato and onion salad.

Serves 4

500 g/1 lb chuck steak, minced
1 onion, grated
salt and freshly ground black pepper
75 g/3 oz Cheddar cheese, grated
150 g/5 oz curd cheese
good pinch dried mixed herbs
1 tbsp tomato purée
8 canned anchovy fillets, drained
½ canned pimiento, drained, cut into
8 strips
8 black olives, halved and stoned
vegetable oil for brushing

These delicious burgers are far more attractive than shop-bought frozen beef burgers which may contain preservative E223, acidity regulator E450(c); flavour enhancer 621, and flavourings.

FISHY · MEALS

Fresh and frozen fish is always available and can be transformed into homemade fish fingers and fish cakes of all shapes and sizes in less time than it takes to go to the supermarket to buy a ready-prepared version.

Frozen fish fingers and fish cakes often contain colourings if they are coated in breadcrumbs. For homemade ones, use home-baked bread for the breadcrumbs – bought bread may contain emulsifiers E471, E472(e) and E481 and brown bread may also contain the preservative E280; while some brands of commercial breadcrumbs contain the colourings E102, E110 and E123.

Breadcrumbs can be made in seconds in a blender or food processor. They can be used as they are or dried in a low oven and stored in an airtight container.

Fish pies and fish in sauce found in supermarket freezer cabinets can contain an assortment of additives such as emulsifiers E322, E471; colouring E102, E110, E142 and E160(b); flavour enhancers 621 and 631 – none of which are needed in a homemade pie.

If buying smoked haddock look for those coloured with the natural colouring crocin, which comes from saffron, rather than the chemical colouring E102. If buying kippers, look for ones coloured with annatto, which comes from the tropical annatto tree, rather than the chemical colour Brown FK (the name stands for Brown for Kippers), which is banned in other European countries. Or look for a fishmonger selling kippers without any colouring at all. They look quite pale, but taste delicious.

Haddock with vermouth and dill

FUN · FISH · CAKES

Heat the oven to 200C/400F/Gas 6. Generously grease a large baking sheet.

Bring the potatoes to the boil in a saucepan of salted water and cook for about 20 minutes until tender when pierced with a knife. Drain and mash.

Meanwhile, put the fish in a large saucepan and cover with cold water. Bring to the boil, then lower the heat and simmer very gently for about 10 minutes.

Remove the fish from the pan with a slotted spoon and cool. Flake the flesh discarding any bones, and mix it very thoroughly with the potato, chives and egg yolk. Season with salt and pepper.

Divide the mixture into 4 equal portions and with floured hands shape into flat pear shapes about 2.5 cm/1 inch thick. Shape the thinner end of the cakes to form a 'V', like the tail of a fish.

Put the egg in a shallow bowl and spread the breadcrumbs out on a flat plate. Dip the cakes in the beaten egg then in the breadcrumbs until thoroughly coated.

Place the fish cakes on the prepared baking sheet, then drizzle the melted margarine evenly over them. Bake in the oven for 20-25 minutes until crisp and golden brown.

To serve: transfer the fish cakes to a serving platter, then place the stuffed olive halves on one side of the fish to represent eyes and garnish with parsley and lemon wedges, if liked.

Serves 4

Variation: Add a little finely grated lemon zest and a few chopped prawns to the mashed potato and fish mixture. Add 2 tbsps grated Parmesan cheese to the breadcrumbs.

350 g/12 oz smoked haddock fillets, skinned
350 g/12 oz potatoes, cut into 2.5 cm/1 inch cubes
2 tbsps snipped chives
1 egg yolk
salt and freshly ground black pepper
3 tbsps plain flour
1 egg, beaten
75 g/3 oz dried breadcrumbs
25 g/1 oz margarine or butter, melted
2 stuffed olives, halved
vegetable oil, for greasing
parsley and lemon wedges, to garnish (optional)

> *Look for smoked haddock with the natural colouring crocin, which comes from saffron, rather than fillets coloured with E102, which is a highly suspect colouring. Make your own breadcrumbs as these can also contain E102 and colourings E110 and E123.*

HADDOCK · WITH · VERMOUTH · AND · DILL

Heat the oven to 170C/325F/Gas 3.

Arrange the haddock pieces in an ovenproof serving dish. Sprinkle over the onion and dill, season with salt and pepper and pour over the stock and vermouth.

Cover the dish with a lid or foil and bake in the oven for 20-30 minutes (30-40 minutes if using frozen fish), or until the fish flakes easily when pierced with a knife.

Pour off the liquid into a small saucepan.

Cover the fish and keep warm in the oven turned down to 110C/225F/Gas ¼. Blend the cornflour with the water in a cup and stir into the liquid in the pan. Bring to the boil, stirring all the time, then season carefully with salt and pepper. Stir in the cream, being careful not to let the mixture boil, and pour over the fish.

Serve at once, garnished with lemon wedges and a few sprigs of dill, if liked.

Serves 4

750 g/1 ½ lb fresh or frozen haddock fillets, skinned and cut into 8 equal-sized pieces
2 spring onions, chopped
1 tsp chopped fresh dill or ½ tsp dried dillweed
salt and freshly ground black pepper
5 tbsps fish or chicken stock (see page 12)
2 tbsps dry vermouth
2 tsps cornflour
2 tbsps water
1-2 tbsps double cream
lemon wedges and dill sprigs, to garnish (optional)

> *Frozen fish in sauce may contain flavour enhancers 621, 631; emulsifiers E322, E471; colourings E142, E102, E160(b). Make your own stock, chicken stock cubes contain flavour enhancers 621 and 635; colouring E150 and also artificial flavouring.*

FISHCAKE · SPECIAL

Bring the potatoes to the boil in a sauce-pan of salted water. Grease an ovenproof plate and arrange the fish fillets on it. Cover with another plate and place on top of the saucepan. Cook for about 20 minutes until the potatoes and fish are tender when pierced with a knife.

Meanwhile, melt 15 g/½ oz butter in a 20-23 cm/8-9 inch frying-pan. Add the onion and fry gently, stirring occasionally, for 5 minutes, until the onion is soft and lightly coloured.

Drain the potatoes and mash them roughly with a potato masher or fork. Flake the fish and fork it through the potato. Stir the onion into the potatoes and fish together with the chopped anchovy fillets, parsley, lemon zest and anchovy essence, if using. Stir thoroughly to mix, then season to taste with salt and pepper.

Melt half the remaining butter and half the oil in the frying-pan. Turn the potato and fish mixture into the pan and, using a fish slice, press down evenly and shape into a round cake. Cook for 8 minutes over moderate heat.

Remove from heat. Place a plate on top of the frying-pan and invert, holding the pan and plate tightly together, to turn the fishcake on to the plate. Scrape out any bits remaining in the bottom of the pan.

Melt the remaining butter and oil in the pan, then using a fish slice, slide the fishcake back into the pan, browned side uppermost. Cook for a further 8 minutes, then carefully transfer to a warmed serving dish. Arrange the anchovy fillets in a trellis pattern on top of the fishcake and garnish with lemon. Serve hot, cut into wedges.

Serves 4

500 g/1 lb plaice fillets, skinned
500 g/1 lb potatoes, cut into 2.5 cm/1 inch cubes
salt
40 g/1½ oz butter
1 onion, chopped
2-3 anchovy fillets, chopped
1 tbsp chopped fresh parsley
finely grated zest of ½ lemon
few drops of anchovy essence (optional)
freshly ground black pepper
1 tbsp vegetable oil
margarine, for greasing
anchovy fillets and lemon slices, to garnish

Ready-to-cook frozen fishcakes often contain emulsifier E450(c) and may also have added co!ourings such as E102 and E124. This mixture makes one large fishcake with no additives.

FISH · FILLET · SANDWICHES

Heat the oven to 230C/450F/Gas 8.

Put the margarine and oil into a 25 cm/10 inch square baking dish and place in the oven to heat.

Divide the cheese into 4 equal portions and on a sheet of greaseproof paper press out to form flat pats slightly smaller than the fish pieces.

Sprinkle the flour over a sheet of greaseproof paper and season with salt and pepper. Lightly beat the egg with the water in a shallow dish. Spread out the breadcrumbs on another sheet of greaseproof paper and sprinkle over the cayenne.

Remove the baking dish from the oven and tip and rotate to swirl the melted margarine and oil evenly over the base of the dish.

Dip 4 of the fish pieces one at a time in the seasoned flour, to coat 1 side only, then coat the same side with the egg mixture and finally with the crumb mixture. Place the coated fish pieces, crumbed sides down, in a single layer in the baking dish. Using a spatula or small fish slice, lift a pat of cheese on to each piece of fish and top with spring onions and pimiento strips.

As in stage 6, flour, egg and crumb the remaining fish pieces on 1 side only, then place them, crumbed sides up, over the fish pieces in the dish. Tip the baking dish and spoon the melted margarine and oil over the tops of the fish sandwiches.

Bake for about 15 minutes, or until the fish will flake easily when tested with a fork, and the crumb coating is golden brown. With a fish slice, carefully remove the fish sandwiches to a warmed serving dish, garnish with parsley sprigs and serve at once.

Serves 4

750 g/1 ½ lb haddock or other white fish fillets, skinned and cut into 8 equal-sized pieces
25 g/1 oz margarine or butter
2 tbsps vegetable oil
75-150 g/3-5 oz Quark soft cheese
25 g/1 oz plain flour, for coating
salt and freshly ground black pepper
1 small egg
1 tbsp water
40 g/1 ½ oz dried breadcrumbs
good pinch of cayenne pepper
2-4 spring onions, finely chopped
1 canned pimiento, cut into thin strips
parsley sprigs, to garnish

Make these delicious fish sandwiches as an alternative to frozen breadcrumbed fish which may contain one or both of the colourings E102, E110, and may also have flavour enhancer 621 added to it.

ORIENTAL · FISH · CURRY

Pour the stock over the desiccated coconut in a bowl and leave it to stand for about 10 minutes.

Meanwhile, heat the oil in a saucepan, add the onion, apple, celery and garlic, if using, and fry for 2 minutes, stirring occasionally. Add the fish to the pan and cook for a further 2-3 minutes, stirring occasionally.

Strain the stock from the coconut. Stir the pimientos, ginger, chilli seasoning and allspice into the pan, then pour in the coconut stock. Bring to the boil, lower the heat, cover and simmer for 10 minutes.

In a small bowl, blend the cornflour to a paste with the water. Stir into the pan, bring to the boil, then lower the heat and simmer until thickened.

Transfer to a warmed serving dish, sprinkle with chopped parsley and serve at once.

Serves 4

750 g/1½ lb coley, filleted, skinned and cut into 2.5 cm/1 inch cubes
300 ml/½ pint fish or chicken stock (see page 12)
2 tbsps desiccated coconut
1 tbsp vegetable oil
1 onion, chopped
1 dessert apple, peeled, cored and chopped
2 celery stalks, chopped
1 garlic clove, crushed (optional)
200 g/7 oz can sweet pimientos, drained and sliced
½ tsp ground ginger
1 tsp chilli seasoning
¼ tsp ground allspice
1½ tbsps cornflour
2 tbsps water
1 tbsp chopped fresh parsley, to garnish

> **Any similar ready-prepared version of this recipe is likely to contain flavourings and colourings such as E150 and E102. Make your own stock as chicken stock cubes contain flavour enhancers 621 and 635; colourings E150 and flavouring.**

BAKED · FISH · FINGERS

Heat the oven to 240C/475F/Gas 9.

Mix together the cornflakes, cheese, herbs and salt and pepper to taste on a sheet of greaseproof paper. Dip the cod into the beaten egg, then coat with the cornflake mixture pressing it on well.

Arrange the cod fingers on a baking sheet lined with aluminium foil. Drizzle a little melted butter over them.

Put the cod fingers into the oven and bake for 10-15 minutes or until the fish feels just tender when tested with a fork and the cornflake coating is golden brown.

Transfer the fish fingers to a warmed serving platter and garnish with watercress sprigs. Serve as a quick lunch with chips and a mixed salad.

Serves 4

500 g/1 lb cod fillet, skinned and cut into 7.5 × 2.5 cm/3 × 1 inch fingers
50 g/2 oz cornflakes, crushed
25 g/1 oz Parmesan cheese, grated
1 tsp dried mixed herbs
salt and freshly ground black pepper
1 large egg, beaten
50 g/2 oz butter, melted
watercress sprigs, to garnish

These fish fingers make a healthier alternative to commercial frozen fish fingers which may contain E102 and E124 and emulsifier E450(c). Look for cornflakes with no artificial colourings or flavourings.

HADDOCK · CASSEROLE

Heat the oil in a flameproof casserole, add the onions and garlic and fry over moderate heat for 10 minutes until browned.

Add the spring onions, green pepper and half the parsley, stir well and fry for 5 minutes, stirring frequently.

Mix the wine with the water and add to the casserole, together with the chopped tomatoes, tomato purée and brandy, if using. Cook for 2 minutes to allow the alcohol to evaporate, then season to taste with salt and pepper. Add the haddock pieces and peeled prawns and stir gently to mix, without breaking up the pieces.

Cover the casserole and continue to cook over moderate heat for 15 minutes until the haddock flakes easily. Remove from the heat, garnish with the unpeeled prawns and remaining parsley and serve at once straight from the casserole, with chunks of bread.

Serves 6

1 kg/2 lb haddock fillet, skinned and cut into 5 cm/2 inch pieces
3 tbsps olive oil or sunflower oil
2 onions, chopped
2 garlic cloves, crushed
4 spring onions, chopped
1 green pepper, deseeded and chopped
4 tbsps chopped fresh parsley
300 ml/½ pint dry white wine
150 ml/¼ pint water
400 g/14 oz can tomatoes, chopped
4 tbsps tomato purée
25 ml/1 fl oz brandy (optional)
salt and freshly ground black pepper
100 g/4 oz peeled prawns
12 unpeeled prawns, to garnish

Look for canned tomatoes without any additives and you have all natural ingredients. Most ready-prepared casseroles have added flavourings and colourings such as E102 and E150.

SALMON · CAKES

Make the dill sauce: in a small bowl combine all the sauce ingredients, reserving a little dill for garnish. Transfer to a small serving dish, cover and chill until ready to serve.

Bring a large saucepan of salted water to the boil, add the rice and cook for about 12 minutes, until just tender. Drain, rinse with cold water and drain again.

Put the drained salmon in a bowl and mash it with a fork. Mix in the cooked rice, grated cheese, Tabasco and the egg yolk, then season to taste with salt and pepper. Divide the mixture into 8 portions and shape each one into a cake.

Lightly whisk the egg white and pour it on to a plate. Put the breadcrumbs on another plate. Dip each salmon cake first in the egg white and then in the breadcrumbs, to coat thoroughly all over.

Pour enough oil into a large frying-pan just to cover the base. Heat the oil, add the salmon cakes and fry for 8-10 minutes, turning once, until golden brown on both sides.

Remove the cakes from the pan with a fish slice and drain on absorbent paper before serving hot, with some of the chilled dill sauce spooned on to each cake and the rest handed separately. Garnish each cake with a sprinkling of the reserved chopped dill over the cream.

Serves 4

215 g/7 ½ oz can pink salmon, drained
75 g/3 oz long-grain rice
75 g/3 oz Cheshire or mild Cheddar cheese, grated
½ tsp Tabasco
1 egg, separated
freshly ground black pepper
50 g/2 oz dried breadcrumbs
vegetable oil, for shallow frying

For the sauce:
150 ml/¼ pint soured cream
2 tsp chopped fresh dill, or 1 tsp dried dillweed
1 tsp lemon juice
salt

Shop-bought fish cakes may contain emulsifier E450(c) and E124. Make your own breadcrumbs as commercial ones may contain the colourings E102, E110 and E123.

GOLDEN · PASTRY · FISH

Put the fish in a saucepan together with the milk, bay leaves and the blade of mace and season with salt and pepper. Bring to the boil, then cover and simmer for 8 minutes until fish is cooked. Strain liquid into a clean saucepan.

In a bowl, blend the cornflour with the lemon juice, then pour on the cooking liquid, stirring all the time. Return to the pan, bring to the boil, then simmer 2 minutes, stirring constantly.

Discard the bay leaves and mace, then remove skin and any bones from the cod and flake the fish with a fork. Add the fish to the prepared sauce together with the prawns, parsley and chives. Adjust seasoning, if necessary. Leave until cold.

Heat the oven to 200C/400F/Gas 6.

Divide the pastry in half, then roll out on a floured surface into 2 strips, 28 × 15 cm/11 x 6 inches for base and 30 × 18 cm/12 × 7 inches for the top. Trim edges of strips.

Place strip for base on a baking sheet, mark into a fish shape with a knife, then cut around the shape. Keep trimmings on one side to use for decoration.

Spread filling evenly over the pastry to within 1 cm/½ inch of edge of fish shape. Dampen the pastry edges and carefully place the lid over the top. Press the edges together really firmly to seal. Trim off any surplus pastry from the lid to match the fish shape of the base. Knock up the edges with the back of a knife and make a decorative border with a fork.

Roll out the pastry trimmings and cut into small rounds with a cocktail biscuit cutter or apple corer. Brush the fish all over with beaten egg, then starting from the tail end, arrange overlapping rounds of pastry all over the fish to look like scales.

With a skewer make a small hole where the eye will go to allow steam to escape. Brush complete surface again with beaten egg.

Bake for 30-35 minutes until the pastry is golden brown and cooked.

Transfer to a warmed serving dish. Place the olive slice over the hole and garnish the pie with the lemon, parsley and whole prawns, if liked.

Serves 4

350 g/12 oz cod fillet
300 ml/½ pint milk
2 bay leaves
blade of mace
salt and freshly ground black pepper
2 tbsps cornflour
2 tbsps lemon juice
100 g/4 oz peeled prawns
1 tbsp chopped parsley
1 tbsp snipped chives
450 g/15 oz shortcrust pastry made
with 300 g/10 oz flour (see Citrus
apple flan page 88)
a little beaten egg, to glaze

For the garnish:
a slice of stuffed green olive
lemon slices
parsley sprigs
unpeeled prawns (optional)

This golden fish pie looks far more glamorous than any commercially produced version and does not contain any of the additives found in the supermarket ones, such as emulsifier E322; colouring E102, E160(b); emulsifying salt E450(a); flavour enhancer 621 and 631.

FISHY · POTS

Pour the milk into a saucepan and heat until simmering. Add the cod and cover the pan. Simmer for 15 minutes or until the fish is cooked. Using a fish slice, transfer the cod to a plate, then flake the flesh with a fork, discarding any bones. Strain the stock into a jug and set aside.

Make the potato topping: put the mashed potato in a bowl, then stir in the butter, milk and nutmeg. Beat until smooth. Season to taste with salt and pepper, then spoon into a large piping bag fitted with a medium-sized nozzle. Set aside.

Melt the butter in a saucepan, sprinkle in the flour and stir over low heat for 1-2 minutes until straw-coloured. Remove from the heat and gradually stir in reserved stock. Return to the heat and simmer, stirring, until thick and smooth.

Stir in the cod. Reserve 4 prawns for the garnish and stir in the rest with the parsley. Simmer gently for 5 minutes and season with salt and pepper.

Heat the grill to high.

Divide the fish mixture equally between 4 small shallow flameproof pots or dishes. Pipe a border of potato around the edge of each pot, then put under the grill for 3-4 minutes, until the potato border has browned a little.

Garnish each pot with a prawn and a sprig of parsley. Serve at once.

Serves 4

250 g/9 oz cod fillets, skinned
300 ml/½ pint milk
25 g/1 oz butter or margarine
25 g/1 oz plain flour
100 g/4 oz frozen peeled prawns, defrosted
2 tbsps chopped fresh parsley
parsley sprigs, to garnish

For the potato topping:
600 g/1¼ lb potatoes, cooked and mashed
25 g/1 oz butter or margarine
2 tbsps milk
pinch of freshly grated nutmeg
salt and freshly ground black pepper

> **Any kind of ready-prepared fish pie may contain flavour enhancer 621 and colourings. These individual fish pies contain all natural ingredients. Serve them with a mixed green salad for a healthy supper dish.**

SPICY · FISH

Put the breadcrumbs in a bowl and stir in the coconut, chilli, coriander and cumin. Season with salt and black pepper to taste.

Spread the flour out on a large flat plate and season with salt and pepper. Beat the eggs in a shallow bowl. Dip the fish strips in the flour, turning to coat thoroughly, then in the egg, and then in the breadcrumb mixture until evenly coated.

Lay the strips on a baking sheet or tray and chill for 10 minutes.

Meanwhile, mix the cucumber and gherkins into the mayonnaise and spoon into a small serving jug; set aside. Heat the oven to 110C/225F/Gas ¼.

Pour enough oil into a deep-fat frier with a basket to come halfway up the sides. Heat the oil to 190C/375F, or until a stale bread cube turns golden in 50 seconds. Fry the fish strips a few at a time for 5-7 minutes until they are golden brown and crisp.

Drain on absorbent paper and keep warm in oven while frying remaining batches. Serve the fish strips at once, garnished with thin wedges of lemon and tomato halves and with the cucumber and gherkin sauce handed separately.

Serves 4

350 g/12 oz rock salmon, bones removed, cut into 10 × 1 cm/4 × ½ inch strips
75 g/3 oz fresh white breadcrumbs
25 g/1 oz desiccated coconut
¼ tsp chilli powder
½ tsp ground coriander
½ tsp ground cumin
salt and freshly ground black pepper
25 g/1 oz plain flour
2 eggs, beaten
¼ cucumber, peeled and chopped
25 g/1 oz gherkins, chopped
6 tbsps mayonnaise
vegetable oil, for deep-frying

For the garnish:
lemon wedges
tomato halves

Make your own breadcrumbs and mayonnaise, then this dish contains all wholesome ingredients. Bought bread may contain the emulsifiers E471, E472(e), E481 and the mayonnaise anti-oxidant E320 and flavourings.

LAYERED · FISH · PANCAKES

Make the pancakes: sift the flour and salt into a bowl, then make a well in the centre. Add the eggs and a little of the milk and whisk together slowly. Pour in the remaining milk and whisk to a smooth batter.

Heat a little butter or oil in a heavy-based 18 cm/7 inch frying-pan over moderate to high heat. Pour off any excess.

Remove the pan from the heat and pour about 1½ tbsps batter into the pan. Return the pan to the heat and cook until the batter is set on the underside. Turn over and lightly cook the other side, then lift on to a sheet of greaseproof paper.

Continue making pancakes in this way, interleaving each with greaseproof paper until you have used all the batter. You should have 10 pancakes.

Heat the oven to 180C/350F/Gas 4.

Make the fish sauce: put the milk into a large shallow pan with the onion slices, bay leaf and peppercorns. Add the fish fillets, bring the milk to the boil, then lower the heat and simmer for 10 minutes.

Lift the fish out of the pan with a slotted spoon and set aside until cool enough to

handle, but not completely cold.

Strain 600 ml/1 pint of the fish cooking liquid into a measuring jug and reserve. Melt the margarine in a clean saucepan, sprinkle in the flour and stir over low heat for 1-2 minutes until straw-coloured. Remove from the heat and gradually stir in the measured liquid. Return to the heat and simmer, stirring, until thick and smooth. Set aside.

Flake the cooked fish, discarding any skin and bones. Pour off 150 ml/¼ pint of the sauce from the pan and reserve. Add the fish to the sauce remaining in the pan, folding it in gently. Add salt and pepper to taste.

Brush a shallow ovenproof dish lightly with butter or oil. Put a pancake on the bottom of the dish, then spread with a little of the mixture. Cover with another pancake, then continue to layer pancakes and sauce in this way until all the ingredients are used.

Spoon the reserved 150 ml/¼ pint sauce over the top of the pancakes and sprinkle with paprika. Bake in the oven for 25 minutes. Serve hot, straight from the dish.

Serves 4

175 g/6 oz plain flour
pinch of salt
2 eggs, beaten
425 ml/¾ pint milk
butter or vegetable oil, for frying and greasing

For the filling:
850 ml/1½ pints milk
2 slices onion
1 bay leaf
10 black peppercorns
750 g/1½ lb haddock fillets (smoked or fresh)
40 g/1½ oz margarine or butter
40 g/1½ oz plain flour
salt and freshly ground black pepper
½ tsp sweet paprika

> **Ready-prepared frozen pancakes with a savoury filling may contain flavour enhancer 621 and colouring E150. If using smoked haddock, look for fillets coloured with the natural colouring crocin which comes from saffron, rather than the colouring E102.**

MARINERS' · FISH · PIE

Heat the oven to 180C/350F/Gas 4.

Mix the fish and shellfish in a bowl with the dillweed and lemon zest and season to taste with salt and pepper.

Melt the margarine in a saucepan, add the onion and fry gently for 5 minutes until soft and lightly coloured. Sprinkle in the flour and stir over low heat for 1-2 minutes. Remove from the heat and gradually stir in the stock. Return to the heat and simmer, stirring, until the sauce has thickened slightly and is smooth. Season to taste with salt and pepper.

Put the fish mixture in a shallow ovenproof dish, about 30 × 14 cm/12 × 5 ½ inches, with a rim, and pour over the sauce. Place a pie funnel or inverted egg cup in the centre of the dish.

Roll out the pastry on a lightly floured surface to a circle that is slightly larger than the top of the dish. Cut a hole in the centre to fit over funnel. Reserve pastry trimmings. Brush the rim of the dish with a little cold water.

Carefully lift the pastry lid on to the dish, press around the edges. Trim off any excess pastry, knock up the edges and flute, then decorate.

Roll out the pastry trimmings and cut into fish shapes. Mark the 'scales' with the point of a small sharp knife. Brush the shapes with water on the unmarked side and press on to the pastry lid.

Mix the egg with a pinch of salt and brush over the pastry lid, to glaze. Bake in the oven for about 40 minutes, until the pastry is golden. Serve at once.

Serves 4

*500 g/1 lb monkfish fillets, skinned
and cut into 2.5 cm/1 inch cubes
100 g/4 oz peeled prawns, defrosted
if frozen
150 g/5 oz can mussels, drained
1 tbsp dried dillweed
grated zest of 1 lemon
salt and freshly ground black pepper
25 g/1 oz margarine or butter
1 onion, chopped
25 g/1 oz plain flour
425 ml/¾ pint fish or chicken stock
(see page 12)
500 g/1 lb puff pastry (see page 75)
1 small egg, beaten*

A ready-made frozen fish pie may contain emulsifier E322; colouring E102, E160(b); flavour enhancers 621 and 631; emulsifying salts E450(a). Make your own puff pastry or look for supermarket fresh or frozen pastry without artificial colourings and flavourings.

FISHY · NOODLE · RING

Heat the oven to 180C/350F/Gas 4.

Bring a large saucepan of salted water to the boil. Add the oil, then the noodles. Bring back to the boil, then lower the heat and simmer for 10-12 minutes until the noodles are tender but firm to the bite.

Meanwhile, whisk the eggs and milk together in a bowl, add the paprika and a pinch of salt.

Use half the melted butter to grease a 1.1 L/2 pint ring mould very generously. Stir the remainder of the melted butter into the egg and milk mixture and pour into the buttered ring mould.

Drain the noodles, then spoon into the ring mould, arranging them evenly around it. Gently fork them into the liquid. Put the ring mould into a large roasting tin and half fill the tin with boiling water. Cook in oven for 40 minutes or until set.

Meanwhile, make the sauce: heat the oil in a saucepan, add the onion and fry gently for 5 minutes until soft and lightly coloured. Add the tomatoes and the purée and cook for about 20 minutes until the sauce is thick. Stir in the basil and the sugar, then season to taste with salt and pepper.

Carefully lower the fish into the pan, stirring to coat the pieces in sauce. Cook for another 5 minutes or until the fish flakes easily when tested with a fork.

To serve: run a knife around the edge of the mould, then invert a warmed serving plate on top. Hold the mould and plate firmly together and invert them, giving a sharp shake halfway round. Lift off the mould. Spoon some of the sauce into the middle and garnish with watercress. Spoon remainder of sauce into a warmed serving dish and hand separately. Serve with a green salad tossed in oil and and vinegar.

Serves 4

175 g/6 oz ribbon noodles
salt
1 tbsp vegetable oil
4 eggs, beaten
300 ml/½ pint milk
¼ tsp sweet paprika
25 g/1 oz butter, melted
watercress sprigs, to garnish

For the fish sauce:
500 g/1 lb cod fillets, skinned and cut into bite-sized pieces
2 tbsps vegetable oil
1 large onion, chopped
750 g/1½ lb tomatoes, skinned and chopped
2 tbsps tomato purée
2 tsps dried basil
½ tsp sugar
freshly ground black pepper

> *Ready-prepared fish and pasta in supermarket freezer cabinets may contain modified starch as a thickening agent; flavouring and flavour enhancers 621 and 631.*

SEAFOOD · MACARONI · BAKE

Squeeze the juice from one-half of the lemon and slice the other half. Grease a large ovenproof dish.

Put the haddock in a large frying-pan with a lid and pour in enough of the milk to just cover. Add 2 slices of lemon, the bay leaf, peppercorns and a good pinch of salt.

Bring gradually to the boil, then cover and turn off the heat under the pan. Leave to stand for 5 minutes, then remove the haddock with a fish slice. Flake the flesh into 4 cm/1½ inch pieces, discarding any bones. Strain all the cooking liquid and reserve for the sauce.

Melt 15 g/½ oz margarine in the rinsed-out frying-pan, add the sliced mushrooms and fry for 2-3 minutes. Stir in the lemon juice and remove from heat.

Heat the oven to 180C/350F/Gas 4.

Put the macaroni into the prepared dish with the haddock, mushrooms and mussels. Stir carefully to mix, without breaking up the fish.

Melt the remaining margarine in a saucepan, sprinkle in the flour and stir over low heat for 1-2 minutes until straw-coloured. Remove from the heat and gradually stir in rest of milk and reserved cooking liquid. Return to the heat and simmer, stirring, until thick and smooth. Remove from heat, stir in the prawns, nutmeg and salt and pepper to taste, then pour evenly over macaroni and fish mixture. Cook in the oven for 20 minutes.

Garnish with lemon slices and unpeeled prawns, if liked, and serve hot, straight from the dish.

Serves 4

350 g/12 oz haddock fillets, skinned
1 lemon
600 ml/1 pint milk
1 bay leaf
3 whole black peppercorns
salt
50 g/2 oz margarine or butter
250 g/9 oz mushrooms, thinly sliced
250 g/9 oz short-cut macaroni, boiled, drained and rinsed in cold water
150 g/5 oz jar mussels, drained
40 g/1½ oz plain flour
250 g/9 oz fresh or frozen peeled prawns
pinch of freshly grated nutmeg
freshly ground black pepper
margarine, for greasing
extra lemon slices and unpeeled prawns, to garnish (optional)

Fish and pasta convenience meals found in supermarket freezer cabinets often contain modified starch as a thickening agent; flavouring and flavour enhancers 621 and 631.

PLAICE · WITH · CREAMY · SAUCE

Heat the oven to 180C/350F/Gas 4.

Roll up the fillets and arrange close together in a small baking dish that will just hold them comfortably in a single layer, side-by-side. Mix together the wine, lemon juice and salt and pepper to taste. Sprinkle over the fillets.

Cover and bake in the oven for 25-30 minutes or until the fish is tender when tested with a fine skewer or knife point.

Using a slotted spoon, transfer the fish to a warmed serving dish. Cover the dish with foil and keep hot in a very low oven.

Pour the cooking liquid into a heavy-based saucepan and bring to the boil. In a small bowl, mix together the cream, egg yolks and mustard. Stir in a little of the hot cooking liquid, then stir this mixture into the liquid in the pan a little at a time, stirring constantly with a wooden spoon.

Continue stirring and cooking very gently until the sauce thickens. Do not boil.

Stir in the capers, then taste and adjust the seasoning.

Pour the sauce over the fish and serve at once, garnished with the parsley sprigs.

Serves 4

4 plaice fillets, skinned
6 tbsps dry white wine
1 tbsp lemon juice
salt and freshly ground black pepper
4 tbsps double cream
2 egg yolks
2 tsps French mustard
2 tsps capers
parsley sprigs, to garnish

The rich creamy sauce for this fish dish contains all natural ingredients. Shop-bought fish in a creamy sauce contains additives such as flavour enhancers 621 and 631; emulsifiers E322 and E471; colouring E142, E102 and E160(b).

FISHY · SURPRISES

Skin and wash the fillets, then dry them on absorbent paper.

Cut the cheese into 8 pieces, each long enough to fit just across the width of a fish fillet. Place a piece of cheese on each fillet and roll it up, starting from the tail end.

Pour the beaten eggs into a shallow dish and put the breadcrumbs on a plate. Coat each fish roll all over in egg, then in breadcrumbs. Repeat, so that the rolls are coated twice, pressing the second coating of breadcrumbs on thoroughly.

Pour enough oil into a deep-fat frier to cover the fish rolls and heat to 170C/325F or until a stale bread cube browns in 75 seconds. Carefully lower the fish rolls into the hot oil and fry for about 7 minutes until they are golden brown and crisp (fry the rolls in 2 batches if necessary). Remove with a slotted spoon and drain on absorbent paper. Serve at once, with tartare sauce.

Serves 4

2 plaice, divided into 8 fillets
100 g/4 oz Cheddar cheese in 1 piece
2 large eggs, beaten
225 g/8 oz fresh white breadcrumbs
vegetable oil, for deep frying

> **If you use homemade bread for the breadcrumbs, this fun version of breadcrumbed fish fillets contains no additives. Frozen bread-crumbed fillets may contain one or both of the colourings E102 and E110 and flavour enhancer 621.**

STUFFED · COD · CUTLETS

Heat the oven to 180C/350F/Gas 4. Grease a shallow ovenproof dish. Cut away the centre bone from each cod cutlet and arrange the cutlets in the dish.

Make the stuffing: mix the oatmeal, parsley, lemon zest and juice in a bowl. Season.

Melt the margarine in a saucepan, add the chopped onion and cook gently for 5 minutes until soft.

Add the onion to the oatmeal mixture in the bowl. Stir in the capers and just enough milk to bind. Using a teaspoon, fill the cavities in the cutlets with stuffing mixture, dividing it equally between them. Sprinkle with grated cheese.

Bake the cutlets in the oven for 20-25 minutes until cooked through.

Serves 4

4 cod cutlets, each about 2.5 cm/1 inch thick
margarine, for greasing

For the stuffing:
2 tbsps medium oatmeal
1 tbsp chopped fresh parsley
finely grated zest and juice of ½ lemon
salt and freshly ground black pepper
50 g/2 oz margarine or butter
1 small onion, chopped
2 tsps capers, drained and chopped
1-2 tbsps milk
50 g/2 oz Cheddar cheese, grated

> **These stuffed cod fillets provide a tasty alternative to frozen fish in a sauce which may contain such additives as flavour enhancers 621 and 631; emulsifiers E322 and E471; colourings E142, E102 and E160(b).**

VEGETABLE · AND · PASTA · DISHES

Canned vegetable and pasta dishes often have artificial thickening in the form of modified starch and may also have colourings and flavourings added. Many have the flavour enhancer monosodium glutamate (621) added to them to disguise the fact that there is very little flavour in the product.

Even canned spaghetti and pasta shapes specificially designed for children and labelled no artificial colours and preservatives often contain monosodium glutamate which can have unpleasant reactions in certain people (see the charts on pages 116-122). and is banned in foods designed for babies and very young children. However, many very young children consume these products.

Quick sauces for pasta dishes are easy to make with natural ingredients, so there is never any need to open a packet sauce mix which may contain additives such as anti-oxidant E320; emulsifiers and stabilizers E471, E472(b); flavour enhancer 621; flavourings; and the synthetic colourings E102, E110 and E124.

Many recipes call for stock and it is well worth making your own (see page 12) and freezing it in 600 ml/1 pint or 300 ml/½ pint quantities so that you always have some handy instead of using a stock cube which will contain several additives such as the flavour enhancers 621 and 635 and the colouring E150.

By making the sauce yourself it is possible to use flavoursome ingredients like fresh vegetables, such as onions, or mushrooms, tomatoes and herbs which have plenty of flavour, so there is no need for flavour enhancers.

Sauces can be cooled, then packed in containers, sealed and frozen. Pack in handy quantities — enough for 1, 2 or 4 servings. They can be reheated from frozen if necessary, so there is always a healthy meal that can be ready in the time it takes to cook the pasta.

Cheesy stuffed aubergines

PARSNIP · AND · NUTMEG · CROQUETTES

Bring the parsnips to the boil in salted water, lower the heat and cook for 20 minutes or until they are very tender.

Drain the parsnips well and then return to the pan and stir over low heat for 1 minute to dry. Add the butter and milk and mash until smooth. Stir in the nutmeg, parsley and egg, then season to taste with pepper. Turn the mixture into a bowl, cover and allow to cool completely for about 1 hour.

Heat the oven to 110C/225F/Gas ¼.

Spread the breadcrumbs out on a plate. With floured hands, divide the parsnip mixture into about 20 equal-sized pieces; roll each piece into a ball. Roll the balls in the breadcrumbs to coat each one thoroughly and evenly all over.

Heat the oil in a deep-fat frier to 190C/375F or until a stale bread cube browns in 50 seconds.

Fry a few of the croquettes for 4-5 minutes until golden brown. Drain on absorbent paper and keep hot in the oven while frying the remaining batches of croquettes.

Sprinkle with grated Cheddar cheese, if liked, and serve.

Serves 4-6

750 g/1½ lb parsnips, cut into 2.5 cm/1 inch chunks
salt
50 g/2 oz butter, diced
1 tbsp milk
¼ tsp freshly grated nutmeg
1 tbsp chopped fresh parsley
1 small egg, lightly beaten
freshly ground black pepper
75 g/3 oz dried breadcrumbs
plain flour, for rolling
vegetable oil, for deep frying
grated Cheddar cheese, for sprinkling (optional)

> **Make your own dried breadcrumbs from homemade bread as commercial ones may contain the colourings E102, E110 and E123. These croquettes can be served around a joint as an accompaniment to chicken or pork chops or as a vegetarian snack.**

CHEESY · STUFFED · AUBERGINES

Trim off stalk end of aubergines, cut aubergines in half lengthways and, leaving a 5 mm/¼ inch thick shell, scoop out and reserve the flesh. Bring a pan of salted water to the boil, add aubergine shells, lower heat and cook for 5 minutes. Lift out and drain the shells upside down.

Heat the oven to 180C/350F/Gas 4. Meanwhile, chop the reserved aubergine flesh. Melt the margarine in a frying-pan, add the onion and fry gently for 5 minutes until soft and lightly coloured. Add chopped aubergine and cook, stirring, for a further 5 minutes until soft.

Remove from heat and mix in the tomato,

breadcrumbs, parsley and half the cheese. Season to taste with salt and pepper. Mix in just enough stock to lightly moisten the mixture without making it sloppy.

Arrange, the drained aubergine shells in a single layer in an ovenproof dish. Spoon the filling into the shells, dividing it equally between them, and sprinkle with remaining cheese. Bake in the oven for 25-30 minutes until the filling is hot and the cheese has melted. Sprinkle with the chopped parsley and serve at once.

Serves 4

2 aubergines, each weighing about 250 g/9 oz
salt
25 g/1 oz margarine or butter
1 onion, chopped
1 tomato, chopped
50 g/2 oz fresh breadcrumbs
1 tbsp chopped fresh parsley
225 g/8 oz mature Cheddar cheese, grated
freshly ground black pepper
1-2 tbsps stock (see page 12)
chopped fresh parsley, to garnish

> **Use homemade bread for the breadcrumbs as commercial crumbs may contain colourings E102, E110 and E123. Make your own stock or use vegetable cooking water, rather than using stock cubes which may contain flavour enhancer 621 and 635; colouring E150 and flavouring.**

CAULIFLOWER · CHEESE · FLAN

Heat the oven to 200C/400F/Gas 6. Place cauliflower florets in a large saucepan and just cover with cold water. Bring to the boil and boil for about 5 minutes. Drain, rinse well under cold water, then drain again very thoroughly and pat dry.

On a lightly floured surface, roll out the pastry and use to line a 20 cm/8 inch plain flan ring on a baking sheet.

Arrange the cauliflower, stalks downwards, in the pastry-lined flan ring. In a bowl, whisk together the milk, eggs and 75 g/3 oz of the cheese, season to taste with salt and pepper and pour it over the cauliflower. Sprinkle evenly with the remaining grated Cheddar cheese.

Cook in the oven for 40-45 minutes until the filling has only just set. Remove from the oven, leave to cool slightly, then carefully remove the flan ring and slide the flan on to a plate. Serve at once, garnished with the tomato slices and watercress sprig, if liked.

Serves 4-6

225 g/8 oz cauliflower florets
250 g/9 oz shortcrust pastry made with 175 g/6 oz flour (see Citrus apple flan, page 88)
225 ml/8 fl oz milk
3 eggs
100 g/4 oz Cheddar cheese, finely grated
salt and freshly ground black pepper

For the garnish:
tomato slices
watercress sprig (optional)

Commercial cheese and vegetable flans may contain such additives as emulsifiers, modified starch as a thickener, and may also contain colourings like E160(b).

WATERCRESS · AND · POTATO · CROQUETTES

Bring the potatoes to the boil in salted water, lower the heat and cook for 20 minutes until tender.

Drain the potatoes and mash with the margarine and milk until smooth. Season to taste with nutmeg, salt and pepper, then beat in the watercress and about one-quarter of the beaten egg. Leave the mixture to cool for about 30 minutes.

On a lightly floured surface, divide the mixture into 12 portions then, with floured hands, roll into cork shapes.

Mix the almonds with the breadcrumbs and spread out on a large flat plate. Dip the croquettes first in the remaining beaten egg, then roll in the almond and bread-crumb mixture. Chill the croquettes for at least 30 minutes.

Heat the oven to 110C/225F/Gas ¼. Heat the vegetable oil in a deep-fat frier to 190C/375F or until a stale bread cube browns in 50 seconds.

Fry a batch of the croquettes in the hot oil for about 5 minutes, until golden brown and crisp, then remove with a slotted spoon and drain on absorbent paper. Keep warm in the oven while frying the rest of the croquettes. Garnish with watercress and serve.

Serves 4-6

750 g/1½ lb potatoes
salt
25 g/1 oz margarine or butter
2 tbsps milk
freshly grated nutmeg
freshly ground black pepper
1 bunch watercress, finely chopped
2 eggs, beaten
flour, for dusting
50 g/2 oz blanched almonds, finely chopped
4 tbsps fresh white breadcrumbs
vegetable oil, for frying
watercress sprigs, to garnish

These croquettes make a tasty alternative to frozen potato croquettes which may contain stabilizer E461 and flavour enhancers 621 and 635. They can be served as a vegetarian snack or as an accompaniment to plainly cooked meat.

FRENCH · BREAD · PIZZAS

Make the tomato sauce: heat the oil in a heavy-based saucepan, add the onion, garlic, if using, and green pepper and fry gently for 5 minutes until the onion is soft.

Add the tomatoes with their juice, the tomato purée, herbs and bay leaf, sugar, celery salt, and season to taste with salt and black pepper. Stir well, bring to the boil, then lower the heat slightly and simmer gently for 20 minutes, stirring occasionally, until tomato sauce is fairly thick and excess liquid has evaporated.

Meanwhile, heat the grill to moderate. Melt the butter in a small saucepan, add the mushrooms and fry gently for 2-3 minutes until tender. Set aside in a warm place.

Cut each half of the bread across into 3 even-sized pieces. Place under the grill, cut-side up, for about 2 minutes until the surface is lightly crisp and evenly coloured.

Divide the tomato sauce between the 6 bread pieces, spreading the sauce over the toasted surface to cover it completely.

Spoon the mushrooms on to the tomato sauce, dividing them equally between the slices of bread, then sprinkle each with the capers. Top with the grated cheese and grill for 10 minutes until cheese bubbles. Garnish with black olives and spring onions, if liked, and serve.

Serves 6

1 large French loaf, cut in half horizontally
25 g/1 oz butter
100 g/4 oz button mushrooms, thinly sliced
25 g/1 oz capers, drained
175 g/6 oz Mozzarella cheese, grated
black olives and spring onions, to garnish (optional)

For the tomato sauce:
1 tbsp vegetable oil
1 onion, thinly sliced
1 garlic clove, crushed (optional)
1 small green pepper, deseeded and thinly sliced
400 g/14 oz can tomatoes
100 g/4 oz tomato purée
1 tsp dried mixed herbs
1 bay leaf
1 tsp sugar
pinch of celery salt
salt and freshly ground black pepper

> **Frozen French bread pizzas may contain emulsifier E472(e), sodium polyphosphates, anti-oxidant E300 and E301; stabilizer E415; and, depending on the topping, they may also contain the preservative E250.**

CARROT · AND · NUT · ROAST

Heat the oven to 180C/350F/Gas 4. Grease an 850 ml/1½ pint shallow oven-proof dish. Grind the nuts and bread together in batches until fairly fine. Tip them into a bowl.

Melt the margarine in a saucepan, add the onion and fry gently for 5 minutes. Add the carrots and cook, stirring, for a further 5 minutes. Add to the nuts and bread in the bowl and mix well together.

Put the hot stock in a bowl, add the yeast extract and honey and stir until dissolved. Stir into the nut mixture with the herbs and lemon juice. Season. Spoon into prepared dish and bake in the oven for 45 minutes. Serve hot or cold.

Serves 4

250 g/9 oz carrots, coarsely grated
100 g/4 oz cashew nuts or pieces
100 g/4 oz walnut pieces
100 g/4 oz wholewheat bread
50 g/2 oz margarine or butter
1 onion, finely chopped
6 tbsps hot vegetable stock
2 tsps yeast extract
1 tsp honey
1 tsp dried mixed herbs
2 tsps lemon juice
salt and freshly ground black pepper
margarine or butter, for greasing

This recipe makes a delicious vegetarian alternative to a processed meat loaf which may contain such additives as flavour enhancer 621; preservative and anti-oxidants.

APPLE · AND · PARSNIP · LAYER

Bring the parsnips to the boil in salted water, lower the heat and cook for 4-5 minutes, until tender. Drain in a colander and rinse with cold water. Drain well.

Heat the oven to 200C/400F/Gas 6 and grease a shallow ovenproof dish. Melt the margarine in a saucepan and fry the onion gently for 5 minutes until soft and lightly coloured. Add apple slices, sage and stock. Cook gently, covered, for 5-7 minutes until the apples are soft. Add salt and pepper to taste and stir to break up the apples.

Arrange one-third of the parsnips in the bottom of the prepared dish and season them with salt and pepper. Sprinkle with

one-third of the cheese and half the walnut pieces, then spread with half the apple sauce. Repeat layers again, then cover with remaining parsnips and top with the remaining cheese. Bake, uncovered, for 30 minutes until the cheese is melted but not browned. Garnish with walnut halves and a parsley sprig, if liked.

Serves 4

500 g/1 lb cooking apples, peeled, cored and sliced thinly
750 g/1½ lb parsnips, cut into 5 mm/¼ inch slices
salt
25 g/1 oz margarine or butter
1 onion, finely chopped
½ tsp dried sage
4 tbsps vegetable or chicken stock (see page 12)
freshly ground black pepper
100 g/4 oz Cheddar cheese, grated
75-100 g/3-4 oz walnut pieces
margarine, for greasing
walnut halves and a parsley sprig, to garnish (optional)

Use homemade stock for this recipe as chicken cubes may contain flavour enhancers 621 and 635, colouring E150 and flavouring. Serve this dish with a green vegetable, or with plain roast or grilled meat.

SPAGHETTI · WITH · TOMATO · SAUCE

Heat the oil in a saucepan, add the onion, garlic, if using, green pepper and mushrooms and fry over moderate heat for about 10 minutes until softened, stirring occasionally during cooking.

Stir the tomatoes with their juice into the softened vegetables, breaking them up with a wooden spoon, and bring to the boil. Lower the heat, add salt and pepper to taste, then simmer for 20 minutes, stirring the sauce mixture occasionally.

Meanwhile, cook the spaghetti in a large pan of boiling salted water for 10-12 minutes or until al dente (tender, yet firm

to the bite). Do not overcook the spaghetti.

Drain the spaghetti thoroughly, then return to the rinsed-out pan. Add the margarine, half the Parmesan, the Italian seasoning and salt and pepper to taste. Toss quickly until all the strands of spaghetti are coated, then transfer to a warmed serving dish.

Taste and adjust the seasoning of the tomato sauce, then immediately pour over the spaghetti and mix well. Sprinkle with the remaining Parmesan and serve at once. Or if you prefer, hand the sauce separately.

Serves 4

500 g/1 lb spaghetti
2 tbsps olive oil
1 onion, chopped
1 garlic clove, crushed (optional)
1 green pepper, deseeded and chop-
ped
100 g/4 oz mushrooms, sliced
2 × 400 g/14 oz cans tomatoes
salt and freshly ground black pepper
25 g/1 oz margarine or butter
50 g/2 oz Parmesan cheese, grated
2 tsps Italian seasoning or dried
mixed herbs

> **Make this simple spaghetti recipe instead of opening a can of ready cooked spaghetti in sauce which may contain some or all of the following additives: modified starch, flavour enhancer 621; even brands labelled free from artificial preservatives and colourings often have flavour enhancer 621. For a high-fibre meal use wholewheat spaghetti and cook it for a few minutes longer.**

PASTA · KUGEL

Heat the oven to 180C/350F/Gas 4. Grease a 1.1 L/2 pint ovenproof dish generously with margarine.

Bring a pan of salted water to the boil and cook the pasta rings for 12 minutes, or according to packet instructions, until they are tender but still firm to the bite.

Meanwhile, beat the eggs in a bowl, add the curd cheese, soured cream and sugar and beat with a fork until smooth. Mix in the raisins, salt and spices.

Drain the cooked pasta rings and return them to the rinsed-out pan. Pour the curd cheese mixture over the pasta and stir it until evenly coated. Transfer the mixture to the prepared dish, sprinkle with chopped mixed nuts and ground cinnamon and dot the surface with the butter.

Bake in the oven, uncovered, for about 30 minutes, until the top is golden and the filling has set around the edge but is still creamy in the middle. Serve at once.

Serves 4

200 g/7 oz wholewheat pasta rings
salt
3 eggs
225 g/8 oz curd cheese
150 ml/¼ pint soured cream
2 tbsps soft brown sugar
100 g/4 oz seedless raisins
¼ tsp ground cinnamon
¼ tsp freshly grated nutmeg
margarine, for greasing

For the topping:
2 tbsps chopped mixed nuts
¼ tsp ground cinnamon
15 g/½ oz butter

Pasta shapes such as rings and shells are always popular with children. Instead of using canned ones, which may contain flavour enhancer, 621, make this wholesome version with no unnecessary additives.

PASTA · PIE

Heat the oven to 200C/400F/Gas 6 and lightly grease a 1.5 L/2 ½ pint pie dish.

Bring a large pan of salted water to the boil, swirl in the oil and add the pasta. Bring back to the boil and then cook for 1 minute only. Drain well and leave to cool while making the fillng for the pie.

Meanwhile, melt the margarine in a saucepan, add the onion and fry for about 3-4 minutes until soft but not coloured. Sprinkle in the flour and stir over low heat for 1-2 minutes until straw-coloured. Remove from heat and gradually stir in the milk. Return to the heat and simmer, stirring, until thick and smooth.

Stir in the chicken and sweetcorn and season with salt and pepper.

Using scissors, cut the pasta into pieces the length of the pie dish. Use two-thirds to line the prepared pie dish, starting at the centre of the dish.

Pour the chicken mixture into the centre of the pasta. Place the rest of the pasta over the top. Sprinkle over the grated cheese and bake in the oven for about 25 minutes.

Serves 4

350 g/12 oz fresh tagliatelle
salt
1 tsp vegetable oil
25 g/1 oz margarine or butter
1 onion, roughly diced
1 tbsp plain flour
300 ml/½ pint milk
250 g/9 oz cooked chicken, diced
200 g/7 oz can sweetcorn, drained
freshly ground black pepper
50 g/2 oz Cheddar cheese, grated
margarine, for greasing

Bulking agents are often added to similar commercial products to make them look more substantial. With a homemade version you know exactly what you've added and there is no unnecessary padding. If fresh tagliatelle is not available, use 175 g/6 oz dried tagliatelle and cook for 7-8 minutes instead of 1 minute.

LAMB · AND · PASTA · MEDLEY

Heat the oil in a saucepan and fry the onion, green pepper and courgettes gently for 2-3 minutes until they are beginning to soften but not brown.

Add the lamb, turn the heat to high and fry until the meat is evenly browned, stirring with a wooden spoon to remove any lumps. Pour off any excess fat.

Stir in the tomatoes with their juice and the water, breaking up the tomatoes with the spoon. Bring to the boil, stirring frequently.

Add the pasta, herbs and salt and pepper to taste and mix well. Cover the pan and simmer the lamb and pasta for 15 minutes.

Stir in mushrooms and simmer, uncovered, for 10 minutes. Sprinkle with the grated Parmesan cheese and serve at once.

Serves 4

Variations: Instead of pasta shapes, use any type of pasta from the store cupboard. Break up spaghetti into small pieces. If using wholewheat pasta, allow a little extra cooking time.

Left-over cooked lamb, finely chopped, may be used, in which case it does not need browning. Alternatively, minced beef can be used instead of lamb.

Dried mixed herbs may be substituted for the dried basil and thyme.

Note: This dish needs no accompaniment as it is a meal in itself.

500 g/1 lb minced raw lamb
2 tbsps olive oil
1 onion, chopped
1 green pepper, deseeded and chop-ped
2 courgettes, finely chopped
400 g/14 oz can tomatoes
300 ml/½ pint water
250 g/9 oz pasta shapes
½ tsp dried basil
½ tsp dried thyme
salt and freshly ground black pepper
100 g/4 oz mushrooms, sliced
1-2 tbsps grated Parmesan cheese, for sprinkling

This pasta and lamb recipe makes a healthy supper dish and is a good alternative to canned pasta shapes in sauce, many of which have the flavour enhancer 621 in them.

DESSERTS

Convenience desserts are some of the products containing the most additives. There are packet desserts of every description – whips and creams, toppings and trifles, cheesecakes and meringue mixes, and in some of them it is hard to find many traces of real food. Often eggs have been replaced by emulsifiers and stabilizers, fruit by synthetic flavouring, then the whole thing is coloured with dye to make it look more acceptable. A typical packet trifle mix from one of the large supermarket chains contains the following:

Emulsifiers: E340, E477
Thickener: E466
Flavourings
Artificial sweetener
Colourings: E102, E110, E122, E123, E124, E127, E132
Anti-oxidant: E320
Preservative: E202

Ready-made desserts

Ready-made fresh and frozen desserts are not quite as bad but most have colourings added – often one of the chemical azo dyes which have been linked with adverse reactions, particularly in children. Many also have flavourings, preservatives and a synthetic cream topping. Imitation cream toppings may be cheaper than real cream but they contain emulsifiers E477, E322; anti-oxidant E320 and colouring E160(a). It is much healthier to eat the real thing or use natural yoghurt. Ice cream is another dessert that is much healthier made at home and the scope for variation is endless. You can use real fruit, or try the delicious brown bread ice cream on page 77. Homemade ones will have none of the additives found in supermarket ice creams (see page 77).

Pastry

Making your own pastry avoids the necessity of eating any of the colourings that may be added to commercial packets of fresh or frozen pastry. Recipes for both shortcrust and puff pastry are included in this chapter (see right and page 88). Shortcrust pastry is so easy to make it is hardly worth buying it ready made. Puff pastry is more time consuming so if you don't like the idea of making it yourself, it is worth looking out for fresh puff pastry which is available in some supermarkets without any additives. This can be frozen for later use. Ready-frozen puff pastry may contain emulsifiers E322, E471 and colouring E160(b).

Quick strawberry cream

PUFF · PASTRY

Sift the flour and salt into a bowl. Add the diced butter and rub it in with your fingertips. Make a well in the centre. Mix 6 tbsps chilled water with the lemon juice and pour into the well. Mix with a fork to give a soft, but not sticky dough, adding the remaining water if necessary.

Turn out the dough on to a lightly floured surface and knead quickly until smooth. Wrap in cling film or foil and refrigerate for 30 minutes. Meanwhile, place the butter between 2 sheets of greaseproof paper and beat it out with a rolling pin into an oblong about 14 × 10 cm/5 ½ × 4 inches and about 1 cm/½ inch thick.

On a lightly floured surface, roll out the dough into a 25 cm/10 inch square. Peel 1 piece of greaseproof paper off the butter. Place the butter in the centre of the dough. Peel off the remaining paper. Fold dough over the long sides of the butter so they slightly over-lap and press seam gently to seal. Fold the short ends inwards, to enclose the butter completely, then press again to seal.

Position the dough so that one of the short sides is towards you. Press the rolling pin gently down on the dough in 3 or 4 places to flatten it slightly, then roll it out into a rectangle 1-2 cm/½-¾ inch thick and 60 cm/24 inches long and 20 cm/8 inches wide (it should be 3 times as long as wide). Roll lightly and evenly away from you and do not take the rolling pin over the edges of the dough.

With the back of a knife, mark out the dough cross-ways into 3 equal portions. Fold the bottom third over the centre, then bring the top third over both. Press the edges to seal with the rolling pin.

Turn the dough round so that a short side faces you. Roll out into a rectangle again but make each side of the rectangle about 2.5 cm/1 inch shorter. Mark into 3 and fold again. Wrap in cling film; chill for 30 minutes.

Repeat the last 3 stages twice more (to make 6 rollings and foldings in all), reducing the size of the rectangle by about 1 cm/½ inch on each edge at each rolling, but still keeping it 3 times as long as wide. After the final folding, wrap in cling film and thoroughly chill the puff pastry for at least 4 hours before using.

Makes about 600 g/1¼ lb

225 g/8 oz strong white flour
pinch of salt
25 g/1 oz butter, diced
6-8 tbsps chilled water
1 tsp lemon juice
200 g/7 oz lightly salted butter

QUICK · STRAWBERRY · CREAM

Beat the cheese with the sugar and vanilla until smooth. Whip the cream until it stands in soft peaks. Fold into the cheese mixture.

Whisk the egg white until stiff, then fold into the cream mixture.

Spoon half the cream mixture into 4 stemmed glasses. Add most of the straw-berries and sprinkle with the orange juice.

Cover with the remaining cream. Decorate with a few strawberry slices and the mint. Serve at once or chill until ready to serve.

Serves 4

250 g/9 oz low-fat soft cheese
25 g/1 oz caster sugar
few drops of vanilla essence
150 ml/¼ pint whipping cream
1 egg white
750 g/1 ½ lb strawberries, hulled and sliced
few drops of orange juice
frosted mint sprigs, to decorate

Make this easy fruit cream, which is full of natural goodness, for a family treat or special occasion, instead of buying a commercial creamy fruit dessert which is likely to have added flavouring, emulsifiers and stabilizers and possibly preservative as well.

STRAWBERRY · YOGHURT · FREEZE

Reserve 6 small strawberries for decoration. Work the remaining strawberries through a nylon sieve, or purée in a blender, then sieve to remove the seeds. Using a fork, stir the yoghurt into the purée until evenly combined with no trace of white.

Sprinkle the gelatine over the water in a small, heavy-based pan. Leave to soak for 5 minutes until spongy, then set over very low heat for 1-2 minutes until the gelatine is completely dissolved. Add the sugar and stir until it is dissolved. Do not allow to boil. Remove from the heat and leave to cool for 5 minutes.

Stir a little of the strawberry yoghurt into the gelatine mixture, then pour on to the bulk of the strawberry yoghurt, stirring all the time until it is well combined.

Pour the mixture into a 1.5 L/2½ pint rigid plastic container, cover and freeze for about 3 hours or until frozen around the edges.

Turn the mixture into a bowl and whisk until smooth. Return to the container, cover and freeze for a further 8 hours, or overnight, until firm.

To serve: transfer the container to the main part of the refrigerator for about 1 hour, or until softened. Spoon into small dishes and decorate with the reserved strawberries. Serve the ices at once, before they start to melt.

Serves 6

500 g/1 lb strawberries, hulled
450 ml/16 fl oz natural yoghurt
1½ tsps powdered gelatine
125 ml/ 4 fl oz water
175 g/6 oz caster sugar

Similar commercial yoghurt and fruit desserts set with gelatine can include stabilizer E466, E412, E415, E410, flavouring and colouring E123.

BROWN · BREAD · ICE · CREAM

Heat the grill to high. Mix the breadcrumbs and sugar together; spread over the base of a small baking tray and toast under the grill for about 5 minutes, turning occasionally, until golden and crunchy.

Turn the crunchy crumbs on to a plate and leave to cool completely, then crush coarsely with the back of a wooden spoon.

Beat the egg yolks with a fork until well blended, then set aside. Whip the cream until it stands in soft peaks.

In a spotlessly clean and dry large bowl, whisk egg whites until stiff. Whisk in brown sugar, 1 tbsp at a time. Using a large metal spoon, fold in the egg yolks, whipped cream, crushed breadcrumbs and dark rum, folding in very gently.

Turn the mixture into a 1.1 L/2 pint metal container and cover securely with foil. Freeze for 2 hours, stirring lightly every 30 minutes to prevent the crumbs sinking, then leave for a further 2 hours, or until firm. (The ice cream can be overwrapped and stored in the freezer for 3 months.)

Let the ice cream stand at room temperature for about 5 minutes, to soften slightly, before serving.

Serves 4

50 g/2 oz fresh wholemeal bread-crumbs
25 g/1 oz sugar
2 large eggs, separated
150 ml/¼ pint double cream
50 g/2 oz light soft brown sugar
1 tbsp dark rum

Commercial ice cream is likely to contain some or all of these additives; emulsifier E471; stabilizers E401, E399 and E466; colourings E104 and E110; flavourings. Chocolate ice cream may contain the colouring Chocolate brown HT, E122 and E124.

CHOCOLATE · MOUSSE

Put the chocolate in a heatproof bowl over a pan of barely simmering water. Heat gently until the chocolate has melted, stirring occasionally.

Remove from the heat and pour the chocolate into a large bowl. Use a flexible spatula to scrape out the last of the chocolate. Leave to cool slightly.

Beat the egg yolks together, then beat

them into the melted chocolate. In a clean dry bowl, whisk the egg whites until they stand in soft peaks. Gently fold them into the chocolate mixture with a spoon.

Spoon the mixture into individual serving dishes, smooth the surface, then chill for 3-4 hours until set. Just before serving, decorate with sugar crystals, if liked.

Serves 4

225 g/8 oz plain dessert chocolate, broken into pieces
4 eggs, separated
coffee sugar crystals, to decorate (optional)

Commercial fresh chocolate mousse may include E471 or E331. Frozen chocolate mousse may include emulsifiers E471 and E322; stabilizer E412; flavouring; colourings E102, E122 and E151.

PINEAPPLE · AND · ORANGE · WHIPS

Trim the pineapple, then cut it across into 8 slices. Cut away the skin and centre core. Cut 1 slice into quarters and reserve for decoration. Chop remaining pineapple flesh into 5 mm /¼ inch pieces.

Finely grate the zest from 1 orange. Peel both oranges, taking care to remove every scrap of bitter white pith. Divide the oranges into segments and remove any pips. Reserve 4 segments for decoration, then coarsely chop the rest.

Whip the cream until it stands in stiff peaks.

Put the cheese, sugar and orange zest into a bowl and beat until pale and very fluffy. Beat in half of the whipped double cream.

In a clean, dry bowl and using clean beaters, whisk the egg white until standing in stiff peaks, then carefully fold into the cheese and cream mixture.

Divide about one-third of the cheese mixture between 4 sundae dishes or stemmed wine glasses, then layer the chopped oranges on top. Spoon half the remaining cheese mixture on top of the layer of oranges.

Divide the pineapple pieces between the dishes, then spoon in the remaining cheese mixture. Top each dish with the remaining whipped cream, cover and chill for 1 hour. (After 1 hour the whips may start to separate, but will still taste delicious.)

To serve: decorate each with the reserved pineapple and orange.

Serves 4

1 small pineapple, weighing about 750 g/1½ lb
2 oranges
150 ml/¼ pint double cream
175 g/6 oz Quark soft cheese
50 g/2 oz caster sugar
1 egg white

> **This whip can be served for a family meal or it is smart enough for a dinner party. For the various additives found in whips see the recipe for Apricot whips below.**

APRICOT · WHIPS

Put the apricots in a small bowl with the hot water and leave to soak for at least 4 hours or, if possible, overnight.

Turn the apricots and water into a heavy-based saucepan. Add the honey, cover and simmer very gently for about 20 minutes, until the apricots are tender. Remove from the heat and leave to cool completely.

Purée the apricots with the cooking syrup and yoghurt in a blender. Alternatively, press the apricots through a nylon sieve, then stir in the cooking syrup and fold in the natural yoghurt until well combined.

Whisk the egg whites until they stand in soft peaks. Using a metal spoon, lightly stir 1 tbsp of the whisked egg whites into the apricot purée mixture, then fold in the remainder.

Spoon the whip into stemmed glasses. Serve at once, or refrigerate until serving time. Serve with the biscuits.

Serves 4

100 g/4 oz dried apricots
300 ml/½ pint hot water
2 tbsps clear honey
300 g/10 oz natural yoghurt
2 egg whites
Carob kisses, to serve (see page 102)

> **Buy dried apricots that have not been treated with sulphur dioxide and you have a totally natural recipe. Commercial whips read like a chemistry directory including some or all of these additives depending on the flavour: emulsifiers E477, E322; gelling agents E339, E450(a); colourings E150, Chocolate brown HT, E100, E102, E160(a); and anti-oxidant E320 so homemade whips are a much healthier alternative.**

COFFEE · CARAMEL · CUSTARDS

Heat the oven to 170C/325F/Gas 3. Rinse out six 150 ml/¼ pint ramekins with very hot water, then stand in a roasting tin and place in the oven to keep hot.

Make the caramel: put the sugar into a heavy-based saucepan with the water. Heat gently, without stirring, until the sugar has dissolved, then bring to the boil and boil rapidly until the syrup turns a light golden colour.

Immediately remove the pan from the heat and plunge the base into cold water. Leave there for a few seconds until the sizzling stops, then remove the pan from the water. Take the roasting tin out of the oven and pour the caramel syrup into the ramekins.

Make the coffee custard: in a large bowl, mix the whole eggs and egg yolks lightly together with a wooden spoon. Stir in the caster sugar. Bring the milk almost to the boil in a small saucepan, then remove from the heat, add the coffee and vanilla and stir until the coffee has dissolved. Slowly stir the milky coffee into the egg and sugar mixture.

Strain the coffee custard into a jug, then slowly pour it into the ramekins. Pour enough hot water into the tin to come halfway up the sides of the ramekins, then bake in the oven for about 45 minutes, or until the point of a knife inserted into the centre leaves a clean cut.

Protecting your hands with oven gloves, lift the ramekins out of the tin and leave to cool. Remove the skin from the surface of the custards, then run a round-bladed knife around the edge of each custard to loosen it slightly, but do not turn out of the ramekins. Chill the caramel custards for at least 2 hours (and up to 4 hours).

To serve: turn out on to individual dishes and serve at once.

Serves 6

2 large whole eggs
2 large egg yolks
40 g/1½ oz caster sugar
600 ml/1 pint milk
3 tbsps instant coffee
¼ tsp vanilla essence

For the caramel:
75 g/3 oz sugar
4 tbsps water

Making custards at home ensures that they include real ingredients like eggs and milk rather than custard powder, flavouring and colours. Commercial caramel custards may include such additives as stabilizers E407 and E401. Packet caramel desserts include gelling agent E339; colourings E102 and E124.

CROWNED · RASPBERRY · JELLY

Place the raspberries and sugar in a small saucepan with the cold water. Bring to the boil, then lower the heat and simmer for 2-3 minutes until mushy. Strain overnight through a jelly bag or muslin.

Measure the raspberry juice and make up to 600 ml/1 pint with water if necessary; set aside 150 ml/¼ pint of the juice. Spoon 2 tbsps of the remaining juice into a small bowl, sprinkle over the gelatine and leave to soak for a few minutes. Set over a saucepan of hot water and heat gently until dissolved, then stir into the larger quantity of raspberry juice.

Pour the jelly into a bowl; cool, then refrigerate until thickened but not set. Rinse out a 1.1 L/2 pint metal jelly mould with cold water, shake off the excess moisture and chill.

Peel and slice the bananas. Turn the slices in the lemon juice, then fold them into the thickened jelly. Spoon into the chilled mould and refrigerate until firm but slightly sticky to the touch. Meanwhile, add the remaining gelatine to the remaining raspberry juice; soak, dissolve and cool.

Whisk the cream into the cool, but still liquid jelly, until evenly mixed and pour over the banana jelly. Chill until the top layer has set. To unmould the jelly: ease edges of jelly away from sides of mould. Dip the mould into a bowl of hot water for 1-2 seconds, then invert a dampened plate on top. Holding mould and plate firmly, invert giving a sharp shake halfway round. Lift off mould. Allow it to stand at room temperature for 30 minutes before serving.

Serves 4-6

750 g/1½ lb fresh or frozen raspberries
100 g/4 oz caster sugar
300 ml/½ pint cold water
5 tsps powdered gelatine
2 small bananas
1 tbsp lemon juice
300 ml/½ pint whipping cream

Jelly tablets contain an assortment of flavourings and colourings according to the flavour of the jelly. Typical colourings are E102, E110 and E124. Other additives include E260, E330 and E331 as well as artificial sweeteners.

RASPBERRY · SOUFFLES

Secure greaseproof paper collars around 4 straight-sided, 175 ml/6 fl oz ramekins. Lightly oil the inside of the paper above the rim of each ramekin.

Work the raspberries through a sieve or purée in a blender, then sieve. This should give 200 ml/7 fl oz purée. Reserve 4 tbsps of the purée.

Sprinkle the gelatine over the water in a cup; leave until spongy, then stand the cup in a bowl of very hot water until the gelatine is completely dissolved.

Meanwhile, whisk the egg yolks and sugar together in a heatproof bowl over barely simmering water until thick and pale.

Remove from the heat. Whisk in the dissolved gelatine and the remaining raspberry purée. Turn into a clean large bowl, cover and chill, stirring occasionally, until on the point of setting.

Whip 225 ml/8 fl oz of the cream until it stands in soft peaks. Using clean beaters, whisk the egg whites until they stand in soft peaks. Fold the cream and egg whites into the raspberry mixture. Divide between the prepared dishes, cover lightly and chill for about 2 hours, until set.

Gently peel away the paper collars with the aid of a round-bladed knife. Press crushed macaroons around the sides.

Sweeten the reserved purée with caster sugar, to taste. Spread 1 tbsp purée over the top of each soufflé.

Whip remaining cream with 2 tsps caster sugar until it stands in soft peaks. Put the whipped cream into a piping bag fitted with a star nozzle. Decorate the top of each soufflé with raspberries and piped cream.

Serves 4

500-600 g/1-1¼ lb fresh or defrosted frozen raspberries
1 tbsp powdered gelatine
3 tbsps cold water
4 large eggs, separated
100 g/4 oz caster sugar
300 ml/½ pint whipping cream
vegetable oil, for greasing
crushed macaroons or Coconut crisps (see page 101),
extra caster sugar and fresh hulled raspberries, to finish

Shop-bought soufflés may contain emulsifiers and stabilizers and synthetic colouring and flavouring. This soufflé contains all natural colourings and flavourings.

JAMAICAN · TRIFLE

Put the brown sugar in a small saucepan with the water and stir over a low heat until dissolved. Bring to the boil and simmer for 4 minutes. Remove from the heat, stir in the rum and leave to cool.

Meanwhile, trim the pineapple, cut off the skin and slice the flesh. Reserve a few slices for decoration; finely chop the rest and put into a bowl. Skin the mango and slice the flesh, discarding the stone. Reserve a few slices; finely chop the rest and mix with the chopped pineapple.

Pour the rum syrup into a shallow dish. Quickly dip half the sponge fingers, one at a time, into the syrup to just moisten them and arrange in the bottom of a glass serving dish. Scatter over half the chopped pineapple and mango. Moisten the rest of the sponge fingers in the rum syrup and arrange on top of the fruit. Scatter over the remaining half of the chopped fruit.

Whip the cream with the caster sugar and vanilla until it holds soft peaks. Spread two-thirds of the cream over the fruit. Pipe or spoon the rest of the cream decoratively on top.

Chill for at least 1 hour, then decorate with the reserved pineapple and mango before serving.

Serves 4

Variation: Other fruits, such as strawberries, raspberries, kiwi fruit and grapes, can be substituted for the pineapple and mango. Medium-dry or sweet sherry can be used instead of the rum, if preferred.

2 tbsps dark soft brown sugar
50 ml/2 fl oz cold water
50 ml/2 fl oz dark rum
1 small pineapple
1 large mango
3-4 slices sponge cake, cut into about 12 fingers
300 ml/½ pint double cream
2 tbsps caster sugar
1 tsp vanilla essence

Packet trifle mixes contain a high number of additives such as E340; thickening agent E466; flavourings; artificial sweeteners; preservative E202; anti-oxidant E320; emulsifiers and stabilizers E466 and E477; and colourings E102, E110, E122, E123, E124, and E127.

GRAPE · MILLE-FEUILLE

Roll out the pastry on a lightly floured surface to a 30 cm/12 inch square. Trim the edges with a sharp knife. Cut square into three 10 cm/4 inch wide strips and place on dampened baking sheets. Prick all over with a fork and chill for at least 10 minutes.

Heat the oven to 220C/425F/Gas 7.

Make the cream filling: whisk the eggs, egg yolks and sugar together until pale and creamy, then gradually whisk in the flour and milk until it is well blended. Pour into a saucepan and bring slowly to the boil, stirring constantly. Lower the heat and simmer for 3-5 minutes until the cream filling is thick and smooth.

Stir in the brandy, then remove from the heat. Pour into a bowl, cover the surface closely with cling film or dampened greaseproof paper and leave to cool.

Bake the pastry in the oven for 10-15 minutes, until risen and golden. Turn strips over and bake 3-5 minutes more to crisp the bases. Place strips on a wire rack and leave them to cool completely.

To assemble: transfer 1 pastry layer to a serving plate. Spread evenly with one-half of the cream filling then arrange one-third of the grapes and kiwi fruit on top. Place another pastry layer on top, then spread over the remaining cream filling and one-third of the fruit. Place the last pastry layer on top and decorate with remaining fruit.

Make the glaze: sieve the jam into a saucepan, stir in the lemon juice and heat until bubbling. Spread carefully over the top layer of fruit. Leave to cool slightly, then chill until ready to serve.

Makes 6 slices

225 g/8 oz puff pastry (see page 75)

For the cream filling:
2 eggs
2 egg yolks
50 g/2 oz caster sugar
50 g/2 oz plain flour, sifted
600 ml/1 pint milk
2 tsps brandy

For the fruit filling and topping:
500 g/1 lb black grapes, halved and with seeds removed
2 kiwi fruit, peeled and sliced

For the glaze:
4 tbsps apricot jam
1 tbsp lemon juice

> **Any commercial pastry containing a creamy filling such as this is likely to have added emulsifiers and stabilizers, as well as synthetic flavouring. Use either homemade puff pastry or look for one that does not contain any synthetic colouring.**

PINEAPPLE · MERINGUE · PIE

Mix the biscuit crumbs with the melted butter. Spoon into a loose-based 20 cm/8 inch sandwich or flan tin and press evenly and firmly over the base and up the sides. Cover and chill for at least 30 minutes.

Heat the oven to 200C/400F/Gas 6. Make the filling: in a small, heavy-based saucepan, mix together the cornflour and sugar. Stir in a little of the reserved pineapple syrup to make a smooth paste, then blend in the remainder. Bring gently to the boil, stirring constantly with a wooden spoon, then remove from the heat.

Allow the mixture to cool slightly, then beat in the egg yolks. Stir in the crushed pineapple. Spoon the pineapple mixture into the biscuit case and level the surface.

In a spotlessly clean, dry bowl, whisk the egg whites until they stand in stiff peaks. Whisk in the caster sugar, 1 tbsp at a time, and continue whisking until the meringue is stiff and glossy. Pipe swirls of meringue over pie or spread with a palette knife, then draw up into peaks. Bake in the oven for 10-15 minutes, until the meringue is golden brown. Leave to cool completely, then remove from the tin and place on a serving plate. Serve at room temperature.

Makes 6 slices

175 g/6 oz digestive biscuits, finely crushed
75 g/3 oz butter, melted

For the filling:
2 tbsps cornflour
2 tbsps sugar
375 g/13 oz can crushed pineapple, well drained, with syrup reserved
2 large eggs, separated
100 g/4 oz caster sugar

A packet meringue mix may contain some or all of these additives: anti-oxidant E320; emulsifier E472(e); colourings E160(e) and E160(a); acidity regulator E336 and E327; stabilizer E412. Look for digestive biscuits without any additives, or use homemade biscuits such as Coconut crisps (see page 101) or Peanut biscuits (see page 105).

LEMONY · CHEESECAKE

Mix the biscuit crumbs with the melted butter. Spoon into a loose-based deep 23 cm/9 inch round cake tin and press over the base. Cover and chill.

Beat the cheese with 1 tbsp milk until smooth and soft. Add the remaining milk together with the sugar, lemon zest, half the lemon juice, the eggs and cream and beat well until smooth. Set aside.

Put the remaining lemon juice in a heat-proof bowl, sprinkle over the gelatine and leave it to soak for 5 minutes until spongy. Stand the bowl in a pan of gently simmering water for 1-2 minutes, stirring occasionally, until the gelatine has dissolved. Remove from the pan and leave to stand for just a few seconds.

Strain the gelatine into the cheese mixture and stir thoroughly. Cover and chill for 30 minutes until the mixture is beginning to set, but is not yet firm.

Stir the cheese mixture well and pour into the tin over the biscuit crust. Cover the tin with cling film and chill for at least 2 hours.

Run a palette knife around the sides of the cheesecake to loosen, then carefully re-move tin. Transfer to a serving plate.

To decorate: heat the lemon curd with the lemon juice until well blended, then set aside until almost cold. Arrange lemon slices on top of cheesecake; spread the lemon curd mixture over the top.

Makes 10 slices

225 g/8 oz digestive biscuits, finely crushed
150 g/5 oz butter, melted

For the filling:
225 g/8 oz Quark soft cheese
150 ml/¼ pint milk
175 g/6 oz caster sugar
finely grated zest of 1 lemon
150 ml/¼ pint lemon juice
2 eggs, beaten
150 ml/¼ pint double cream
150 ml/¼ pint single cream
1 rounded tbsp (1 sachet) powdered gelatine

For the decoration:
2 tbsps lemon curd (see page 114)
1 tbsp lemon juice
lemon slices, peeled

Look for digestive biscuits without additives — brands vary. Shop-bought cheesecake may contain emulsifiers E475, E471; colourings E102 and E110 and flavouring.

BLACK · CHERRY · CHEESECAKE

Mix together the biscuit crumbs, ground almonds and melted butter. Spoon into a loose-bottomed 20 cm/8 inch flan tin or shallow cake tin and press evenly over the base. Cover and chill for about 30 minutes, until firm.

Make the filling: beat the cheese with honey to taste until smooth and creamy, then spread it evenly over the biscuit base.

Drain the cherries well, reserving 8 tbsps syrup from the can. Halve and stone the cherries and arrange them, cut side down, over the soft cheese.

In a small saucepan, blend the cornflour to a smooth paste with the reserved cherry syrup. Add the redcurrant jelly and lemon juice and stir until well mixed. Bring the mixture slowly to the boil, stirring constantly with a wooden spoon, then simmer for 1-2 minutes until thick.

Remove the pan from the heat and spoon the hot glaze over the cherries, covering them completely. Leave until cold and set. Just before serving, decorate the top with flaked almonds.

Makes 6-8 slices

150 g/5 oz digestive biscuits, finely crushed
25 g/1 oz ground almonds
75 g/3 oz butter, melted

For the filling:
175 g/6 oz Quark soft cheese
1-2 tsps clear honey
425 g/15 oz can black cherries
2 tsps cornflour
2 tbsps redcurrant jelly
1 tbsp lemon juice
flaked almonds, to decorate

Packet cheesecake mixes may contain anti-oxidant 320; emulsifiers and stabilizers E401, E472(b) and E475; colourings E102 and E124; flavouring and modified starch.

CITRUS · APPLE · FLAN

To make the pastry: sift the flour and salt into a large bowl. Cut the margarine into 1 cm/½ inch cubes, add to the flour and rub in until the mixture resembles coarse crumbs. Sprinkle over the water, then draw the mixture together to a firm dough. Wrap in cling film and chill for at least 30 minutes before using.

Heat the oven to 200C/400F/Gas 6.

Roll out the pastry on a floured surface and use to line a 20 cm/8 inch loose-based sandwich tin or a plain or fluted flan ring placed on a baking sheet. Prick lightly in several places with a fork.

To make the filling: in a saucepan, melt the margarine over low heat. Remove the pan from the heat and stir in the sugar, breadcrumbs, grated orange zest and ground mixed spice.

Spread marmalade over the base of the flan. Peel, core and slice the apples and arrange over the marmalade. Spoon the breadcrumb mixture evenly over the top and press down lightly.

Bake in the oven for 25 minutes, then reduce the heat to 180C/350F/Gas 4 and bake for a further 10-15 minutes until it is golden brown.

Remove from the tin, sift icing sugar lightly and evenly over the top of the flan to dust. Transfer to a warmed serving plate and serve the flan hot.

Serves 4

175 g/6 oz plain flour
pinch of salt
75 g/3 oz margarine or butter
2 tbsps water, chilled

For the filling:
75 g/3 oz margarine or butter
75 g/3 oz caster sugar
100 g/4 oz fresh breadcrumbs
grated zest of 1 orange
½ tsp ground mixed spice
4 tbsps marmalade (see page 115)
2 cooking apples
icing sugar, to dust

Make your own pastry and use homemade bread for the breadcrumbs and you avoid the need for any additives. Commercial pastry may have added colouring E102 and flavouring. Supermarket bread may include emulsifiers E471, E472(e) and E481 and preservatives E280 and E281. Commercial apple flans may include modified starch as a thickening agent and stabilizer E401.

LATTICED · GOOSEBERRY · TART

Heat the oven to 200C/400F/Gas 6.

Cut off one-third of the pastry and reserve. On a lightly floured surface, roll out the remaining pastry and use to line a 23 cm/9 inch pie plate.

Mix the gooseberries with the breadcrumbs, sugar and mint, if using. Spoon into the pastry-lined pie plate and spread evenly. Brush the edges of the pastry with water.

Roll out the reserved pastry to a rectangle 1 cm/½ inch larger than diameter of the pie plate. Cut into 1 cm/½ inch wide strips and use to make a lattice decoration over the tart. Brush the pastry lattice with beaten egg.

Bake the tart in the oven, just above the centre, for 20 minutes; then lower the heat to 190C/375F/Gas 5 and bake for about 15 minutes more, until the gooseberries are tender. Cover the top with greaseproof paper if the pastry is browning too quickly.

Remove the tart from the oven and sift caster sugar thickly over the top. Serve hot, warm or cold, with custard or cream.

Serves 4

350 g/12 oz shortcrust pastry made with 225g/8 oz flour (see Citrus apple flan, see opposite)
little beaten egg, for glazing
caster sugar, for dredging
custard or cream, to serve

For the filling:
225 g/8 oz gooseberries, topped and tailed if fresh, defrosted and well drained if frozen
2 tbsps fresh white breadcrumbs
25 g/1 oz sugar
½ tsp finely chopped fresh mint
(optional)

Make your own pastry and use homemade bread for the breadcrumbs and you avoid the need for any additives. Commercial pastry may have added colouring E102 and flavouring. Supermarket bread may include emulsifiers E471, E472(e), E481 and preservatives E280 and E281. Commercial gooseberry tarts may include modified starch as a thickening agent and stabilizer E401.

APRICOT · AND · WALNUT · SPONGE

Generously grease an 850 ml/1½ pint pudding basin. Cut a circle of greaseproof paper or foil 7.5 cm/3 inches larger all round than the basin top. Grease 1 side, then make a 1 cm/½ inch pleat down the centre. Reserve.

Wash the apricots and cut them into small pieces with scissors.

Cream the margarine or butter with the sugar until light and fluffy. Add the beaten eggs a little at a time, beating in after each addition. Thoroughly stir in a few drops of almond essence.

Sift together the flour and salt, then, using a metal spoon, lightly fold into the creamed mixture alternately with the apricots and walnuts. Stir in the milk.

Spoon the mixture into the prepared pudding basin. Level the surface. Place the reserved pleated greaseproof paper, greased side down, on top of the basin, then secure in place with string.

Place the basin in a large, heavy-based saucepan and pour in enough hot water to come halfway up the sides of the basin. Bring the water slowly to the boil, then lower the heat until the water is simmering. Cover the pan with a well-fitting lid and steam the pudding for 1½ hours or until well risen and firm to the touch on top. Top up with more boiling water if necessary.

Protecting your hands with oven gloves, carefully lift the basin out of the pan. Allow the pudding to stand, still covered, for 5 minutes before turning out.

Meanwhile, melt the jam in a small saucepan with lemon juice to taste, stirring constantly to mix.

To serve: remove the paper from the pudding, then turn out on to a warmed serving plate. Pour the melted jam over the pudding and serve at once while still piping hot.

Serves 6

100 g/4 oz tenderised dried apricots
100 g/4 oz margarine or butter
100 g/4 oz caster sugar
2 eggs, lightly beaten
few drops of almond essence
175 g/6 oz self-raising flour
pinch of salt
50 g/2 oz shelled walnuts, roughly chopped
2 tbsps milk
margarine or butter, for greasing

To serve:
4-5 tbsps apricot jam
a little lemon juice, to taste

Shop-bought fruit sponge puddings may include emulsifier E471, stabilizers E415, 410 and 412. Look for dried apricots that have not been treated with sulphur dioxide.

MAGIC · CAROB · PUDDING

Heat the oven to 190C/375F/Gas 5. Lightly grease a 1.5 L/2½ pint fairly deep oven-proof pie dish.

Sift flour into a bowl with carob powder and salt, then set aside.

Beat the margarine and caster sugar together until pale and fluffy, then beat in the vanilla. Beat in the eggs, a little at a time, adding 1 tbsp of the flour mixture with the last few additions of egg. Gradually stir in the remaining flour mixture and mix well, then add just enough milk to give the mixture a smooth dropping consistency; do not make too runny.

Spoon the mixture into the prepared dish, spread it evenly and level the surface.

Make the sauce: mix together the brown sugar and carob powder, then gradually blend in the water, stirring vigorously to avoid lumps. Pour the sauce over the mixture in the pie dish.

Bake just above the centre of the oven for 40 minutes, or until the pudding is well risen and browned and the carob sauce beneath is syrupy. Serve the pudding hot straight from the dish.

Serves 4

75 g/3 oz self-raising flour
2 tbsps carob powder
pinch of salt
100 g/4 oz margarine or butter, softened
100 g/4 oz caster sugar
¼ tsp vanilla essence
2 eggs, lightly beaten
1-2 tbsps milk
margarine, for greasing

For the sauce:
100 g/4 oz light soft brown sugar
2 tbsps carob powder
300 ml/½ pint boiling water

Commercial puddings similar to this one may contain emulsifiers and stabilizers, as well as synthetic colourings and flavourings. This pudding contains only natural flavouring.

CUSTARD · TART

To make the pastry: sift the flour and salt into a bowl and stir in the sugar. Make a well in the centre. Cut the margarine into 1 cm/½ inch cubes and put in the well with the egg yolk and water. With the fingers of one hand, gradually work the dry ingredients into centre until evenly mixed, then form into a ball of fairly firm dough. Wrap in cling film and chill for 30 minutes.

Heat the oven to 200C/400F/Gas 6.

Roll out the pastry on a lightly floured surface and use it to line a 20 cm/8 inch loose-bottomed flan tin or flan ring placed on a baking sheet. Chill for 30 minutes.

Prick the base of the pastry case with a fork, line with greaseproof paper and weight down with baking beans. Bake in the oven for 10 minutes.

Beat the egg white lightly. Remove the pastry case from the oven, take off the paper and beans and brush with the beaten egg white. Return the pastry case to the oven and bake for a further 5 minutes.

Meanwhile, make the custard filling: beat the eggs in a bowl and whisk in the sugar and vanilla essence. Bring milk almost to boiling point in a small saucepan, then whisk into the eggs. Strain the mixture into a jug.

Pour the custard mixture into the hot pastry case and sprinkle with grated nutmeg, covering the custard.

Reduce the oven temperature to 170C/325F/Gas 3 and bake the tart for 30 minutes, or until the custard is just firm in the middle and will part cleanly if cut with a knife. Lift off the sides of the flan tin or remove the ring and return to the oven for a further 5 minutes to crisp the pastry. Serve warm or cold.

Serves 4

100 g/4 oz plain flour
pinch of salt
15 g/½ oz caster sugar
65 g/2 ½ oz margarine or butter
1 egg, separated
1 tsp cold water

For the custard filling:
2 eggs
25 g/1 oz caster sugar
few drops of vanilla essence
300 ml/½ pint milk
½ tsp freshly grated nutmeg, or to taste

> **Even fresh shop-bought custard tarts made with eggs and milk may contain extra flavouring and colouring such as E160. This recipe uses all wholesome ingredients and does not require artificial flavouring.**

JAM · ROLY · POLY

Heat the oven to 200C/400F/Gas 6.

Sift the flour and salt into a bowl. Rub in the margarine, then add enough water to make a firm dough.

Turn the dough out on to a lightly floured surface and knead briefly, then roll out to form a 25 × 20 cm/10 × 8 inch rectangle. Trim the edges to straighten.

Spread the jam to within 2 cm/¾ inch of the edges, then turn in the edges so that they line up with the jam, then pinch the corners together. Starting at one short edge, roll the dough up, like a Swiss roll.

Grease a piece of foil. Carefully lift the roll on to the foil. Bring the long edges up over the roll and crimp together to seal, leaving room for the roll to expand. Crimp the side edges of the roll together.

Place on a baking tray and cook in oven for 1¼ hours. Open the foil about 10 minutes before the end of the cooking time to let the roll brown slightly. Serve at once.

Serves 6

Note: Serve with a jam sauce made by heating 4 tbsps jam with 300 ml/½ pint orange juice or white wine.

225 g/8 oz self-raising flour
pinch of salt
100 g/4 oz cold margarine, cubed
100 ml/3 ½ fl oz water
4 tbsps blackcurrant jam
butter, for greasing

A shop-bought roly poly may contain emulsifiers and stabilizers, as well as flavouring and colourings. Use homemade jam and you have a tasty dessert without the need for synthetic flavouring.

BREAD · BISCUITS · AND · CAKES

When you think how a homemade sponge cake starts to go stale after 2 or 3 days, you can see how many additives must be needed to keep a similar cake on the supermarket shelf for several weeks without it deteriorating at all. The following are the type of additives that might be found in cakes; stabilizer E401, E470, E471; colourings E150, E102, E110; preservatives E202, E220; gelling agent E440(a), acidity regulator E330; and flavouring.

If on the other hand you feel it is very handy to have a packet cake mix in your store cupboard, bear in mind some of their additives such as:

Anti-caking agent E341
Colourings: E171, E150, E124
Stabilizer: E466
Anti-oxidants: E320, E321
Emulsifiers: E471, E475
Flavourings
Sodium aluminium phosphates

The most wholesome ingredients in the cake — eggs and milk — usually have to be added by the consumer when making the cake.

Biscuits
These have some of the same additives as cakes, such as anti-oxidant E320; flavourings; colouring E150.

Bread
Both brown and white bread may contain emulsifiers E471, E472(e) and E481. White bread is likely to be made with bleached flour which destroys the vitamin E and other nutrients. Wholemeal flour is not bleached, so bread made with this type of flour does not contain bleach but preservatives E280 and E281 are usually added to inhibit mould. Some brands have no preservative added if sold in a large supermarket but may have them added if sold elsewhere. Shop-bought brown or white bread may contain 920, 924, 926, 927 or E300 as flour improvers.

It is possible to buy unbleached white flour which is suitable for bread or pastry making, but it is not widely available. One large supermarket chain is looking into the possibility of selling it but has no definite plans so far.

Cheese, celery and peanut loaf

WHITE · LOAF

Sift the flour and salt into a warmed large bowl. Rub in the fat, then stir in the yeast until well blended. Pour in the tepid water and mix to a soft, slightly sticky dough which leaves the sides of the bowl cleanly.

Turn the dough out on to a lightly floured surface and knead vigorously for about 10 minutes until smooth and elastic and no longer sticky. Shape the dough into a ball and place it in an oiled large bowl. Cover with oiled polythene and leave to rise in a warm place for about 1¼ hours, or until the dough has doubled in bulk.

Turn the dough out on to a lightly floured surface and knead for 1 minute. Grease a 1.7L/3 pint (a 1 kg/2 lb) loaf tin. Flatten the dough into an oblong about 38 × 23 cm/15 × 9 inches: fold it in 3 to make an oblong 23 × 13 cm/9 × 5 inches and fold the short ends inwards. Place seam-side down in the oiled tin. Cover with oiled polythene and leave to prove until the dough has almost reached the top of the tin. Meanwhile, heat the oven to 230C/450F/Gas 8.

Bake the dough in the oven for 30-40 minutes until the bread is golden and just shrinking from the sides of the tin. Turn out the bread and rap the underside with your knuckles — if cooked it should sound hollow. If not cooked return the bread, on its side, to the oven and bake a few minutes longer. Cool on a wire rack.

Makes 1 large loaf

750 g/1½ lb strong white flour
1½ tsps salt
15 g/½ oz margarine or butter
7 g/¼ oz sachet easy-blend dried yeast
450 ml/¾ pint tepid water
vegetable oil, for greasing

Use non-bleached white flour if you can find it in a health food shop. Commercial white loaves contain emulsifiers E471, E472(e) and E481.

CHEESE · CELERY · AND · PEANUT · LOAF

Mix the sugar and yeast with the water and leave in a warm place for 10 minutes until frothy. Grease base and sides of a loaf tin measuring about 20 × 10 cm/8 × 4 inches across the top and 6 cm/2¼ inches deep. Set aside in a warm place.

Place the flour and salt in a bowl and rub in the margarine or butter until the mixture resembles breadcrumbs. Stir in the mustard, celery, cheese and yeast liquid and mix to a dough.

Turn the dough out on to a floured surface and knead for 5 minutes,then place in the prepared tin and press gently to fit the shape. Cover the tin with oiled polythene and leave in a warm place for about 1¼ hours, or until the dough has risen and doubled in size. Meanwhile, heat the oven to 200C/400F/Gas 6.

Uncover the loaf and brush the top with beaten egg, then sprinkle with the chopped peanuts. Bake in the oven for about 40 minutes or until cooked. To test that the loaf is cooked, turn it out of the tin and rap the underside with your knuckles: it should sound hollow. If not cooked return the bread on its side to the oven and bake a few minutes longer. Place the loaf on a wire rack and leave to cool completely.

This loaf is best served very fresh. It is delicious thickly sliced and buttered.

Makes 12 slices

Note: This loaf is ideal for freezing. Wrap the cold loaf in a polythene bag, seal, label and freeze for up to 4 weeks. To serve: unwrap the loaf and allow to defrost for 2-3 hours.

1 tsp light soft brown sugar
1 tsp dried yeast
185 ml/6 ½ fl oz tepid water
275 g/10 oz wholewheat flour
1 tsp salt
25 g/1 oz margarine or butter
1 tsp mustard powder
1 celery stalk, very finely chopped
50 g/2 oz mature Cheddar cheese, finely grated
little beaten egg, for glazing
1 tbsp chopped salted peanuts
vegetable oil, for greasing

This delicious cheesy loaf is free from any of the additives found in commercial breads such as emulsifiers E471, E472(e) and E481; and preservatives E280 and E281.

FLOWERPOT · LOAF

Season a clean, unused earthenware flowerpot measuring 13 cm/5 ½ inches across the top and 12 cm/5 inches tall. Brush the inside with oil, then place in a 200C/400F/Gas 6 oven for 15 minutes. Leave to cool.

Mix the flours together in a large bowl with the salt. Rub in the margarine, then sprinkle in the yeast and stir well to mix. Pour in the water and mix to a firm dough.

Turn the dough out on to a floured surface and knead for 10 minutes, or until it is smooth and elastic and no longer sticky, then shape it into a round.

Brush the inside of the seasoned pot very thoroughly with oil, then sprinkle in 2 tsps bulgur wheat.

Place the dough in the prepared pot, pressing it down well. Cover with oiled polythene and leave in a warm place for about 1¼ hours, or until the dough has risen just above the top of the flowerpot.

Heat the oven to 230C/450F/Gas 8.

Uncover the dough and brush the top with milk. Sprinkle over the remaining bulgur wheat and press it down lightly. Bake the loaf in the oven for 30-35 minutes until the top of the loaf is browned and crusty.

Cool the loaf for 2-3 minutes, then run a palette knife around the sides to loosen it. Turn the loaf out of the pot, then place the right way up on a wire rack and leave to cool completely before cutting into slices.

Makes 8-10 slices

175 g/6 oz strong white flour
175 g/6 oz strong wholewheat flour
1 tsp salt
15 g/½ oz margarine, diced
1 tsp easy-blend dried yeast
200 ml/7 fl oz hand-hot water
1 tbsp bulgur wheat
milk, for glazing
vegetable oil, for greasing

Most shop-bought bread contains an assortment of additives. White loaves may contain emulsifiers E471, E472(e), E481. Many brown breads contain emulsifier E472(e) and preservatives E280 and E281 which inhibit mould (these are less likely to be used in white bread as the flour has usually been bleached).

VIENNA · ROLLS

Sift the flour and salt into a warmed large bowl. Rub in the margarine, then stir in the yeast. Make a well in the centre. Mix the milk with the water and pour into the well, then mix to a firm dough.

Turn the dough out on to a lightly floured surface and knead for 10 minutes until smooth and elastic, then form into a ball. Clean and grease the bowl. Return the dough to the bowl and turn it over to coat the surface lightly with oil. Cover the bowl with oiled polythene and leave to rise in a warm place for about 1 hour, or until the dough is doubled in bulk.

Grease 2 baking sheets or trays thoroughly with vegetable oil.

Turn the dough out on to a lightly floured surface and knead for 2 minutes. Divide the dough into 12 pieces, then roll out each to 15 × 7.5 cm/6 × 3 inches oval. Roll up tightly from one long side, then place seam-side down on a baking sheet. Make 11 more rolls spacing well apart. Slash diagonally on top. Cover with oiled polythene and leave to rise in a warm place for 30 minutes, or until doubled in size.

Meanwhile, heat the oven to 230C/450F/Gas 8. Place a roasting tin in bottom of oven and pour in enough boiling water to come halfway up sides.

Uncover the rolls and bake in centre and just above centre of oven for 10 minutes. Remove the tin of water. Allow steam to escape from oven. Brush top and sides of rolls with cream, then sprinkle with poppy or caraway seeds, if liked.

Return to the oven, swapping the sheets, for a further 10 minutes, or until the rolls are rich golden brown and shiny. Transfer to a wire rack and leave to cool.

Makes 12

750 g/1½ lb strong white flour
2 tsps salt
25 g/1 oz margarine, diced
7 g/¼ oz sachet easy-blend dried yeast
225 ml/8 fl oz warm milk
200 ml/7 fl oz hand-hot water
50 ml/2 fl oz single cream or high-cream milk, for glazing
poppy or caraway seeds (optional)
vegetable oil, for greasing

Like many other white loaves, supermarket Vienna rolls and loaves often contain emulsifiers E471, E472(e) and E481. These homemade rolls are not only free of additives but they also have a lovely soft crust.

SYRUP TEA BREAD

Heat the oven to 180C/350F/Gas 4. Grease a 1.75 L/3 pint (1 kg/2 lb) loaf tin, line the base with greaseproof paper, then grease the paper.

Sift the flour, baking powder and soda into a bowl, then stir in the chopped dates and the raisins.

Put the syrup, sugar, milk and margarine into a heavy-based saucepan. Heat gently, stirring frequently with a wooden spoon, until the sugar has dissolved and the margarine has melted. Do not allow to become hot. Remove from the heat and pour on to the flour mixture, then beat with the spoon until the ingredients are evenly and thoroughly blended.

Spoon the mixture into the prepared tin and level the surface. Bake in the oven for 1-1¼ hours, or until the bread is risen, browned and firm to the touch. Cover with greaseproof paper, if necessary, to prevent the top overbrowning.

Cool the bread for 5 minutes, then run a palette knife around the sides to loosen it and turn out of the tin. Peel off the lining paper. Leave on a wire rack to cool completely. Serve sliced, with plenty of butter.

Makes 12-14 slices

350 g/12 oz plain flour
1 tbsp baking powder
½ tsp bicarbonate of soda
50 g/2 oz stoned dates, chopped
50 g/2 oz seedless raisins
100 g/4 oz golden syrup
50 g/2 oz light soft brown sugar
300 ml/½ pint milk
50 g/2 oz margarine
vegetable oil, for greasing
butter, to serve

This delicious syrup tea bread makes a good alternative to bought tea buns which may contain various additives such as emulsifiers E471 and E472(e), and modified starch. The bread can be cut as soon as it is cold and is best eaten within 3 days.

ICED · WALNUT · TEA · RING

Mix the sugar and yeast with the water and leave in a warm place for 10 minutes until frothy. Brush a baking sheet with oil.

Place the flour and salt in a bowl and rub in the margarine or butter until the mixture resembles breadcrumbs. Stir in the yeast and sugar mixture.

Turn the dough out on to a floured surface and knead for 5 minutes. Roll out to a rectangle about 35 × 20 cm/14 × 8 inches. Brush with the melted butter, then sprinkle with the chopped nuts and caster sugar. Starting from one long side, neatly roll up the dough. Dampen the ends and join them together firmly to make a ring.

Place the ring on the oiled baking sheet. Using scissors, snip the ring at 2.5 cm/1 inch intervals to within 2 cm/¾ inch of the centre, without cutting through, so that the filling shows.

Cover with oiled polythene and leave to rise in a warm place for about 1 hour, or until almost doubled in size. Meanwhile, heat the oven to 220C/425F/Gas 7.

Uncover the ring and bake in the oven for 15 minutes; reduce the oven temperature to 180C/350F/Gas 4 and bake for a further 15 minutes, or until golden brown. Place on a wire rack and leave to cool.

Blend the icing sugar with enough orange juice to give a coating consistency. Spoon over the ring, then arrange the walnut halves on top and sprinkle over the orange zest. Leave to set.

Makes 8-10 slices

1 tsp light soft brown sugar
1 tsp dried yeast
185 ml/6 ½ fl oz tepid water
275 g/10 oz wholewheat flour
1 tsp salt
25 g/1 oz margarine or butter
25 g/1 oz butter, melted
50 g/2 oz shelled walnuts, finely chopped
25 g/1 oz caster sugar
100 g/4 oz icing sugar, sifted
about 5 tsps orange juice
vegetable oil, for greasing

For the decoration:
8 walnut halves
grated zest of 1 orange

Iced buns bought in the supermarket can contain emulsifiers E471 and E482, and artificial flavourings. Walnuts and very finely grated orange zest make a very pretty decoration and are much healthier than glacé cherries, which contain the colouring E127, or artificially coloured icing.

JAP · CAKES

Heat the oven to 140C/275F/Gas 1. Line 2 baking sheets with pieces of non-stick vegetable parchment paper or lightly oiled greaseproof paper.

In a clean, dry bowl, whisk the egg whites until standing in stiff peaks. Whisk in the sugar, 1 tbsp at a time, and continue to whisk until meringue is stiff and glossy. Fold in ground almonds.

Put the mixture into a piping bag fitted with a large plain nozzle. Pipe twenty 5 cm/2 inch rounds on to baking sheets, spacing them about 2.5 cm/1 inch apart.

Bake below the centre of the oven for 1-1¼ hours, until firm and crisp. Swap sheets halfway through baking. Peel the paper off the rounds while warm, then leave to cool completely.

Make the buttercream: sift the icing sugar with the carob. Beat the butter until very soft, then slowly beat in the sugar mixture and water.

Sandwich the rounds in pairs with buttercream, then chill for 15-20 minutes to firm.

Hold each biscuit on its side and dip into the melted chocolate so that one edge is coated, giving a crescent effect. Leave on a wire rack to set before serving.

Makes 10

2 large egg whites
100 g/4 oz caster sugar
75 g/3 oz ground almonds
50 g/2 oz plain dessert chocolate, melted, to finish

For the buttercream:
50 g/2 oz icing sugar
2 tsps carob powder
25 g/1 oz butter, softened
1 tsp hot water

These chocolate-dipped biscuits make ideal party treats. Commercially produced biscuits with a similar buttercream filling would be likely to contain additives such as colouring E150 and flavourings.

GARIBALDI · BISCUITS

Heat the oven to 200C/400F/Gas 6. Grease a large baking sheet.

Sift the flour and salt into a bowl, then stir in the sugar. Add the margarine and rub it in with your fingertips until the mixture resembles fine breadcrumbs. Add 2 tbsps milk and mix to a fairly firm dough.

Turn the dough out on to a lightly floured surface and knead briefly until smooth, then roll out to a 23 cm/9 inch square.

Cut the dough in half with a sharp knife. Brush one half generously with milk and sprinkle evenly with the currants. Place the remaining piece of dough on top and press down lightly. The milk makes the work surface sticky, so clean and flour it again before rolling out the dough.

Roll out to a rectangle, about 25 × 20 cm/10 × 8 inches. Trim the edges with a sharp knife, then cut into 24 fingers. Brush the tops generously with beaten egg.

Using a palette knife, place the biscuits, just touching, on the prepared baking sheet. Bake in the oven, just above the centre, for 10-12 minutes, until browned. Use the oven timer if you have one, as it is very easy to overbake these biscuits.

Let the biscuits settle for a few seconds, then transfer to a wire rack and leave to cool completely. Break apart to serve.

Makes 24

100 g/4 oz self-raising flour
pinch of salt
25 g/1 oz caster sugar
40 g/1½ oz margarine or butter, diced
about 3 tbsps milk
50 g/2 oz currants
beaten egg, to glaze
margarine or butter, for greasing

Garibaldi biscuits on the supermarket shelf may contain emulsifier E322 and anti-oxidant E320.

COCONUT · CRISPS

Heat the oven to 180C/350F/Gas 4. Grease 2 large baking sheets. Sift the flour, salt and cinnamon into a bowl. Add the caster sugar, margarine and egg. Mix well, then beat for 1-2 minutes. Mix in the coconut.

Roll 1 heaped tsp of the mixture into a ball, then place on a prepared baking sheet and flatten slightly with a fork. Continue in this way until all the mixture is used up, spacing the biscuits 2.5 cm/1 inch apart.

Bake in the oven for 15-20 minutes until golden. Swap the sheets halfway through baking. Let the biscuits settle for a few seconds, then transfer to a wire rack to cool completely.

Makes 28

100 g/4 oz self-raising flour
pinch of salt
1 tsp ground cinnamon
100 g/4 oz caster sugar
100 g/4 oz soft tub margarine
1 egg
75 g/3 oz desiccated coconut
vegetable oil, for greasing

Similar shop-bought coconut biscuits may contain several of the following: raising agents sodium bicarbonate, E334, ammonium bicarbonate, anti-oxidant E320, and flavouring.

CHEESE · BISCUITS

Heat the oven to 200C/400F/Gas 6. Lightly grease a baking sheet. Sift the flour.

In a large bowl, beat the butter until pale and creamy, then beat in the cheese. Add the flour a little at a time, beating thoroughly after each addition, to form a stiff dough.

Sprinkle the sesame seeds on a lightly floured work surface and roll out the dough until about 2 mm/⅛ inch thick. Cut the dough into about 12 rounds using a lightly floured 7.5 cm/3 inch pastry cutter.

Using a palette knife, transfer the rounds to the prepared baking sheet, spacing them apart, then bake for 5-8 minutes until golden brown. Let the biscuits settle for 1-2 minutes, then transfer to a wire rack and allow to cool.

Makes about 12

Variation: These biscuits can be cut into straws or into fancy shapes using petits fours cutters. They make ideal nibbles for drinks parties.

100 g/4 oz mature Cheddar cheese, grated
100 g/4 oz wholewheat flour
100 g/4 oz butter, softened
2 tbsps sesame seeds
margarine, for greasing

> **Many shop-bought savoury biscuits contain the colouring E150 as well as flavourings. These biscuits make the ideal accompaniment to pâtés and dips instead of crisps which contain numerous additives.**

CAROB · KISSES

Heat the oven to 190C/375F/Gas 5. Grease a large baking sheet. Beat the margarine and icing sugar together until fluffy. Sift the flour and carob powder into a separate bowl. Using a hand-held electric whisk or a wooden spoon, work the flour into the sugar to make a soft dough.

Put the dough into a piping bag fitted with a large star nozzle and pipe about 30 small rosettes on to the baking sheet. Bake the biscuits in the oven for 15 minutes, or until firm and set underneath. Cool on the baking sheet for 5 minutes, then transfer to a wire rack to cool.

Meanwhile, make the filling: beat the margarine and icing sugar together until pale and fluffy, then beat in the orange zest and juice. Sandwich kisses with filling. Sift icing sugar lightly over the top and serve the biscuits within 1 – 2 hours.

Makes about 15

175 g/6 oz margarine or butter, softened
50 g/2 oz icing sugar
175 g/6 oz plain flour
25 g/1 oz carob powder
vegetable oil, for greasing
icing sugar, to finish

For the orange filling:
50 g/2 oz margarine or butter, softened
100 g/4 oz icing sugar
grated zest of 1 orange
1 tsp orange juice

> **These light, crispy biscuits are made with carob powder rather than cocoa powder as cocoa powder contains synthetic flavouring. Carob powder is prepared from the fruit of the carob tree. It is higher in iron than cocoa powder, while lower in fat and sodium. It is used in the same quantities.**

SPICED · BLACKCURRANT · BARS

Heat the oven to 180C/350F/Gas 4. Lightly grease a shallow 30 × 18 cm/12 × 7 inch cake tin, line the base with greaseproof paper and grease the paper with margarine.

Beat the margarine and sugar until pale and fluffy. Add the syrup and egg, a little at a time, beating thoroughly with a wooden spoon after each addition.

Sift the flour, baking powder and mixed spice together, then fold into the creamed syrup and egg mixture a little at a time.

Spread two-thirds of the mixture into the prepared tin. Spread over the jam and then spoon remaining mixture on top and spread it as evenly as possible with the back of the spoon. (Spooning the mixture into the tin and then spreading it helps prevent it mixing in with the jam. It is not necessary to completely cover the jam as the mixture spreads during cooking.) Sprinkle over the walnuts and bake just above centre of the oven for about 35-40 minutes until golden.

Leave to cool in the tin, then cut into 16 slices. The spiced bars can be stored in an airtight container for 2 – 3 days.

Makes 16 slices

100 g/4 oz margarine
150 g/5 oz caster sugar
50 g/2 oz golden syrup
1 egg, beaten
225 g/8 oz plain flour
1 tsp baking powder
2 tsps ground mixed spice
225 g/8 oz blackcurrant jam
5 g/3 oz walnut pieces, finely chopped
margarine, for greasing

Similar shop-bought biscuits often contain preservatives, flavourings and colourings, so it is a much healthier alternative to make these spiced bars at home with no extra additives.

CUSTARD · CREAMS

Heat the oven to 170C/325F/Gas 3. Grease 2 baking sheets or trays.

Sift the flours into a bowl. In a separate large bowl, beat the butter and caster sugar together until pale and fluffy. Beat in the egg, a little at a time, then gradually work in the flour mixture to make a firm and smooth dough.

Turn the dough out on to a lightly floured surface and knead briefly, then roll it out to a 25 cm/10 inch circle. Using a plain or fluted 4 cm/1½ inch round cutter, cut the dough into as many rounds as possible. Knead the trimmings together, roll out again and cut into more rounds until there are 28 altogether.

Place the rounds on the prepared baking sheets and prick well with a fork. Bake on centre shelf and just above for 20-25 minutes, until lightly browned. Swap the sheets halfway through baking. Cool the biscuits for a few seconds, then loosen them with a palette knife and transfer to a wire rack. Leave to cool completely.

Meanwhile, make the filling: beat the butter until very soft and creamy, then gradually beat in the icing sugar. Add the lemon juice, 1 teaspoon at a time, and beat well until smoothly blended.

Sandwich the biscuits in pairs with the creamy filling and serve them as soon as possible.

Makes 14

50 g/2 oz self-raising flour
50 g/2 oz cornflour
50 g/2 oz butter or margarine, softened
50 g/2 oz caster sugar
1 egg yolk, lightly beaten
vegetable oil, for greasing

For the filling:
15 g/½ oz butter or margarine, softened
25 g/1 oz icing sugar, sifted
2 tsps lemon juice

Commercial custard creams contain flavouring and colouring E160(b). The cream filling may also contain additives such as anti-oxidants. This recipe if made with butter contains no additives, and if made with margarine contains only harmless ones.

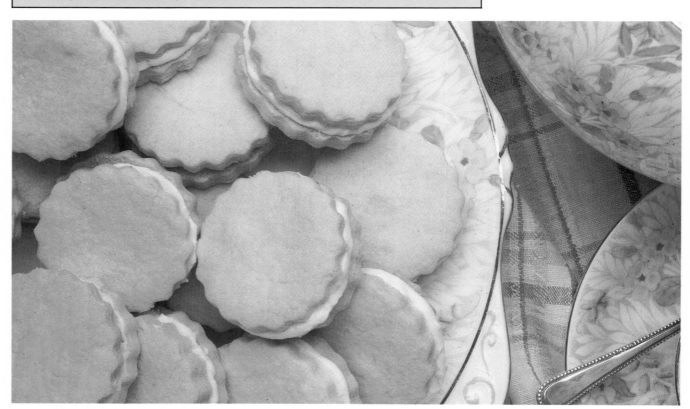

PEANUT · BISCUITS

Heat the oven to 190C/375F/Gas 5. Prepare several baking sheets. Lightly flour non-stick sheets; butter and then flour others.

Sift the flour with the bicarbonate of soda. Grind 75 g/3 oz peanuts in a blender or clean coffee grinder.

Beat the butter to a cream. Add the sugar and beat until fluffy. Beat in the egg. Stir in the flour and ground peanuts.

Form mixture into teaspoon-sized balls and then place on to the prepared baking sheets, 5 cm/2 inches apart. Flatten them slightly with a wet fork and put a half peanut in the centre of each of the flattened shapes.

Bake the biscuits, in batches if necessary, for 8-10 minutes. Keep a careful eye on them because they burn easily.

Cool them for 5 minutes on the baking sheets, then lift them with a palette knife or fish slice on to wire racks and leave to cool completely before serving.

Makes about 45-50

175 g/6 oz plain flour
½ tsp bicarbonate of soda
75 g/3 oz peanuts, unsalted
75 g/3 oz butter, softened
175 g/6 oz light soft brown sugar
1 egg, beaten
additional 50 g/2 oz peanuts, halved, to decorate

With these delicious peanut biscuits there is no need for added artificial flavourings of the kind found in many supermarket varieties. Shop-bought biscuits like these often contain anti-oxidant E320 as well.

RASPBERRY · CREAM · CAKE

Heat the oven to 170C/325F/Gas 3. Grease the bases of two 18 cm/7 inch round sandwich tins. Line them with greaseproof paper, then lightly grease the paper with melted margarine.

Sift the flour and baking powder into a large bowl. Add the soft margarine, caster sugar, eggs and vanilla essence and beat vigorously for 2-3 minutes until blended.

Divide the mixture equally between the prepared tins, level each surface and make a shallow hollow in the centre. Bake in the oven for 25 minutes until just firm to the touch when lightly pressed.

Let the cakes stand in the tins for a few minutes. Lay a clean tea-towel on a wire rack, then turn out the cakes. Peel off lining paper. Turn them the right way up, then leave to cool completely.

Make the filling: whip the cream until stiff. Lightly crush the raspberries and fold them into the whipped cream.

Spread 1 cake with half the jam, then with the raspberry cream filling. Spread the underside of the other cake evenly with the remaining jam. Cut it into 6-8 wedges, then position these one at a time, jam-side-down, on top of the raspberry filling. Place them slightly apart so the filling shows through. Sift icing sugar thickly over the top of the cake.

Makes 6-8 slices

100 g/4 oz self-raising flour
1 tsp baking powder
100 g/4 oz soft tub margarine
100 g/4 oz caster sugar
2 large eggs, beaten
1-2 drops vanilla essence
melted margarine, for greasing
icing sugar to dredge

For the filling:
150 ml/¼ pint whipping cream
100 g/4 oz fresh or frozen raspberries, defrosted if frozen
4-6 tbsps raspberry jam

This delicious cake has none of the additives found in a shop-bought version with fresh fruit and cream, such as stabilizer E401, modified starch and flavouring. Make your own jam or look for one with no added colourings or flavourings.

SHERRY · LAYER · CAKE

Heat the oven to 180C/350F/Gas 4. Grease two 4 cm/1½ inch deep, 18 cm/ 7 inch round tins. Line each base with greaseproof paper, then lightly grease the paper with melted margarine.

Sift the flour into a large bowl. Add the sugar, margarine, eggs and orange zest and beat with a wooden spoon for 2-3 minutes until evenly and smoothly blended.

Divide the mixture equally between the prepared tins and level each surface. Stand the tins on a baking sheet, then bake in the oven for 35-40 minutes, or until the cakes are springy to the touch.

Cool the cakes for 1-2 minutes, then turn out of the tins and peel off the lining paper. Place the cakes, the right way up, on a wire rack and leave to cool completely.

Make the icing: beat the butter until very soft, then slowly beat in the icing sugar.

Continue beating until the mixture is pale and creamy, then beat in the sherry until it is well combined.

Assemble the cake: place 1 cake on a serving plate. Mix together the sherry and orange juice and spoon half evenly over cake. Spread one-third of the icing over the cake, then top with the second cake. Sprinkle with the remaining sherry and orange mixture. Spread top with half of remaining icing, leaving a 5 mm/¼ inch border around the edge. Mark a wavy pattern very lightly in the topping with a small palette knife.

Place remaining icing in a piping bag fitted with a small star nozzle and pipe a border of small rosettes around top edge of cake. Refrigerate for 20-25 minutes to firm. Just before serving, decorate the top of the cake with frosted flowers.

Makes 10-12 slices

175 g/6 oz self-raising flour
175 g/6 oz caster sugar
175 g/6 oz block margarine at room temperature
3 eggs
finely grated zest of 1 orange
2 tbsps sweet sherry
2 tbsps orange juice
extra margarine, melted for greasing

For the sherry butter icing:
75 g/3 oz butter, softened
225 g/8 oz icing sugar, sifted
2 tbsps sweet sherry
frosted flowers, for decoration

A packet of cake mix for a sponge with buttercream filling may contain a real 'additive cocktail' of emulsifiers E471, E475; flavourings; anti-caking agent E341; anti-oxidants E320 and E321, and colourings depending on the flavour of the cake. Make your own frosted flowers instead of using sugar flowers which contain guar gum, hyfoama, and colourings E102, E127, E122, E110, E132. Simply brush non-poisonous petals with beaten egg white, sprinkle with caster sugar and leave to dry.

FRUITY · SLAB · CAKE

Heat the oven to 180C/350F/Gas 4. Lightly grease a shallow 27 × 18 cm/11 × 7 inch cake tin. Line the base and sides with greaseproof paper so that the paper extends about 2.5 cm/1 inch above the sides of the tin. Grease the paper.

Sift the flour, baking powder, spice and salt into a large bowl. Add the margarine and rub it in with your fingertips until the mixture resembles fine breadcrumbs.

Stir in the sugar, dried fruit and treacle. Beat the eggs and milk together, then gradually stir them into the mixture, to give a soft dropping consistency.

Turn the mixture into the tin and level the surface. Bake in the oven for 45-50 minutes until golden and firm to the touch and a skewer inserted in the centre comes out clean.

Holding the greaseproof firmly, lift the cake on to a wire rack. When cool, but not cold, turn it over on to your hand and quickly peel off the greaseproof paper. Return the cake to the rack, the right way up.

Leave on the wire rack until cold, then serve cut into squares.

Makes 12 squares

350 g/12 oz plain flour
1 tbsp baking powder
1 tsp ground mixed spice
1 tsp salt
150 g/5 oz margarine or butter, diced
150 g/5 oz sugar
75 g/3 oz raisins
75 g/3 oz sultanas
1 tsp black treacle
2 eggs
225 ml/8 fl oz milk
melted margarine, for greasing

Many shop-bought fruit cakes contain glacé cherries with colouring E127, mixed peel with preservatives E202 and E220, and may also have the colourings E102 and/or E110 added.

OLD-FASHIONED · SEED · CAKE

Heat the oven to 170C/325F/Gas 3. Grease a 1.75 L/3 pint (1 kg/2 lb) loaf tin. Line the tin with greaseproof paper, then grease the paper.

Sift the flours with the salt. In a separate bowl, beat the butter and sugar until very pale and fluffy. Add the eggs, a little at a time, beating the mixture thoroughly after each addition.

Using a large metal spoon, fold in the sifted flours, then stir in milk. Add the caraway seeds and gently fold them in, making sure they are evenly distributed. Turn the mixture into the prepared tin and level the surface, then make a shallow hollow in the centre. Sprinkle the sugar over the top.

Bake in the oven for 1-1¼ hours, or until firm to the touch and a warmed fine skewer inserted into the centre of the cake comes out clean. Cover with greaseproof paper, if necessary, towards the end of cooking to prevent overbrowning.

Cool the cake for 10-15 minutes, then turn out of the tin and peel off the lining paper. Place the cake the right way up on a wire rack and then leave to cool completely before slicing and serving.

Makes 12 slices

100 g/4 oz plain flour
100 g/4 oz self-raising flour
pinch of salt
175 g/6 oz butter, softened
175 g/6 oz caster sugar
3 large eggs, lightly beaten
2 tbsps milk
2 tsps caraway seeds
2 tbsps sugar, to finish
vegetable oil, for greasing

Nearly all commercially produced cakes similar to this old-fashioned English recipe contain colourings such as E102 and E110, and may also have added preservative E200.

JAMS · PICKLES · AND · PRESERVES

Jams, preserves, chutneys and pickles are easy to make at home and they avoid the necessity of eating a varied range of colourings and flavourings found in many supermarket preserves. Some manufacturers are now producing jams and marmalades without artificial colourings and flavourings though these may still have additives like acidity regulators. Others contain some of the most suspect colourings such as E102 and E124 which are azo dyes (see the charts on pp 116-122 for their possible adverse effects).

The colourings are quite unnecessary and are simply added because manufacturers think that customers will only buy brightly coloured jam.

Similarly, if good quality fruit is used, there is no need for any chemical flavouring; the fruit will provide enough flavour.

Commercial chutneys may also contain E102 or E150, another colouring that is causing concern. They often have flavour enhancer 621 added as

well. If you make your own chutneys with good quality ingredients you will find they have an excellent flavour without any need for artificial flavour enhancers. Pickles may have additives like artificial sweeteners, preservatives and colourings.

Try substituting different herbs and spices to vary the flavour.

Use fresh fruit, preferably slightly under-ripe as the pectin content is higher then. Virtually any kind of fruit can be made into jam, and all sorts of interesting ones can be be made using combinations of fruit and also some vegetables, such as marrows and carrots.

When the fruit has a high-pectin content 700 g/1½ lb sugar can be added to 500 g/1 lb fruit; if medium-pectin content, then 500 g/1 lb sugar for 500 g/1 lb fruit. If the fruit has a low pectin content then just adding sugar will not set it and pectin or acid in the form of lemon juice must be added.

Marrow and ginger jam

STRAWBERRY · CONSERVE

Cut any large strawberries in half. Put the fruit into a preserving pan or large heavy-based stainless steel or aluminium pan. Sprinkle over half the sugar and mix gently, then cover and leave for at least 12 hours or overnight.

Heat the oven to 110C/225F/Gas ¼. Wash and rinse the jam jars. Drain. Spread the remaining sugar in a large baking tray and place in the oven to warm. Meanwhile, add the lemon juice to the strawberries. Set over low heat and simmer gently, stirring frequently, for 20-30 minutes, until the fruit is very soft.

Clip a sugar thermometer (if using) to the sides of the pan. Add the warmed sugar and the butter. Stir over low heat until the sugar is dissolved. Bring quickly to the boil and boil rapidly until the thermometer registers 105C/221F and a set is reached.

To test for a set, remove the pan from the heat, spoon a few drops of jam on to a cold saucer, allow to cool, then push a finger gently through it. If the surface of the jam wrinkles, setting point has been reached. If not, boil the jam for a further few minutes and repeat the testing for a set.

Remove the pan from the heat and skim off any scum with a slotted spoon. Cool the jam for 45 minutes, then stir gently and ladle into the dry jars. The jam will still be very runny at this stage. Wipe the rims and outsides of the jars with a clean, damp cloth. Place waxed paper discs on top of the jam. Leave to cool completely, then cover with jam pot covers and secure with rubber bands.

Label, then store in a cool, dry place.

Makes about 2 kg/4 ½ lb

1.75 kg/3 ½ lb strawberries, hulled
1.4 kg/3 lb sugar
3 tbsps lemon juice
knob of butter

> **Commercial strawberry jam may have several additives such as colouring E124, acidity regulator sodium citrate and preservative E226. This jam contains only natural ingredients.**

MARROW · AND · GINGER · JAM

Remove the skin from the marrow, then cut it in half and scoop out the seeds. Cut the flesh into 5 mm/¼ inch dice, place in a colander and sprinkle with salt. Put a plate on top, weight down and leave overnight or for about 12 hours.

Rinse the marrow under cold running water and pat dry with absorbent paper.

Put the marrow in a bowl with the sugar, cover with a cloth and leave for a further 12 hours.

Heat the oven to 110C/225F/Gas ¼. Wash and rinse the jam jars. Drain, then stand them on a baking sheet and place in the oven to warm.

Transfer the marrow and sugar to a preserving pan or a very large aluminium or stainless steel saucepan and add the lemon zest and juice and ginger. Cook over low heat for about 10 minutes until the marrow is transparent then test for a set as for Strawberry conserve.

At once pour the jam into the warmed jars, filling them right to the top. Place waxed paper discs on top of the jam while still very hot, then cover with jam pot covers and secure with rubber bands.

Label the jars and store in a cool, dry place.

Makes about 1.5 kg/3 ½ lb

1 kg/2 lb marrow
salt
1 kg/2 lb sugar
finely grated zest and juice of 1 lemon
100 g/4 oz crystallized ginger, coarsely chopped

> **Making your own marrow and ginger jam avoids the possibility of eating any artificial colourings and flavourings which may be added to a commercial version.**

GRAPEFRUIT · CURD

Heat the oven to 110C/225F/Gas ¼. Wash and rinse 4-6 small jars. Drain, then stand them on a baking sheet and place in the oven to warm.

Pour enough water into the bottom pan of a double boiler to come halfway up the sides of the pan. If you do not have a double boiler, use a large, heavy-based saucepan and medium-sized heatproof bowl which will sit snugly on top. Bring to the boil, then lower the heat slightly so the water is just simmering.

Put the eggs into the top pan of the boiler and beat lightly together with a wooden spoon. Stir in the citrus zest, juice, sugar and butter.

Set the mixture over the simmering water.

Stir until the butter has melted and the sugar has dissolved, then cook for 40-50 minutes, stirring occasionally, until the curd is thick enough to coat the back of the spoon.

Pour the grapefruit curd into the warm jars. Place waxed paper discs on top, then cover with jam pot covers and secure with rubber bands. Leave to cool completely, then store in a cool, dry place. Use within 1 month.

Makes about 1 kg/2 lb

Variation: For lemon curd use the grated zest and juice of 4 lemons instead of the grapefruit.

finely grated zest and juice of 1 grapefruit
4 large eggs
finely grated zest of 1 lemon
3 tbsps lemon juice
500 g/1 lb caster sugar
100 g/4 oz butter, diced

Grapefruit curd, which is not readily available commercially, has a more delicate flavour than lemon curd and is just as easy to make. A variation is given for lemon curd which is much healthier made at home. Supermarket lemon curd may contain several of the following: colourings E102, E110, E124; preservative E220; and modified starch.

CLEMENTINE · MARMALADE

Heat the oven to 110C/225F/Gas ¼. Wash and rinse the jam jars. Drain, then stand them on a baking sheet and place in the oven to warm.

Pour the water into a preserving pan or large heavy-based saucepan.

Wash all the fruit. Remove peel and pith from grapefruit and lemons and chop finely. Chop flesh and place peel and flesh in pan. Cut clementines in half, pull all the flesh away from peel and put flesh in pan.

Cut clementine peel into fine, short shreds and put into a piece of clean muslin about 30 cm/12 inches square, bringing sides of muslin up to enclose them. Tie securely. Put bag into pan and bring water and fruit to boil, reduce heat and simmer gently for 45 minutes.

Remove bag, untie and turn shreds into a nylon sieve. Rinse in cold water and drain thoroughly on absorbent paper. Set aside.

Continue cooking the marmalade for 1½ hours, then add sugar and stir over low heat until the sugar has dissolved completely. Clip a sugar thermometer, if using, to the pan. Add the rinsed clementine shreds and bring to the boil.

Boil marmalade at full rolling boil for 20 minutes, or until sugar thermometer registers 105C/221F and a set is reached. Test for a set as for Strawberry conserve (see page 113).

When set is reached, remove pan from heat and skim the scum from the surface. Leave marmalade for 20-30 minutes, then slowly pour the marmalade into the jam jars. Cover jars with waxed paper discs, leave to cool, then cover with jam pot covers and secure with rubber bands. Label the jars and store in a cool, dry place.

Makes 2.3 kg/5 lb

1 kg/2 lb clementines
2.8 L/5 pints cold water
1 tsp citric acid
350 g/12 oz grapefruit
250 g/8 oz lemons
1.4 kg/3 lb sugar

Marmalade in the supermarket may contain one or more of the following additives: colouring E150; emulsifier E331; gelling agent E440(a). This tasty marmalade can be made without any additives.

GREEN · TOMATO · CHUTNEY

Put all the ingredients in an enamelled or stainless steel saucepan and heat gently, stirring, until the sugar has dissolved.

Bring to the boil, then lower the heat slightly and simmer for 2 hours, stirring occasionally until the liquid has evaporated and the tomatoes are pulped.

Meanwhile, select jars with vinegar-proof lids. Heat the oven to 110C/225F/Gas ¼. Wash and rinse the jam jars. Drain, then stand them on a baking sheet and place in the oven to warm.

Pour the hot chutney into the prepared jars. Cover with waxed paper discs while still hot and seal tightly with the vinegar-proof lids. Leave until completely cold.

Label and store chutney for at least 2 months before using.

Makes about 2.5 kg/5 lb

Note: This is an excellent way to use green tomatoes when they are plentiful and inexpensive at the end of the tomato season.

For the jars, use preserving jars with lids, or Kilner jars. Alternatively, use glass, screw-top coffee jars which have plastic-lined lids.

This hot-tasting chutney adds a zing to cold snacks or complements all types of curries.

2 kg/4 ½ lb green tomatoes, chopped
500 g/1 lb onions, chopped
250 g/9 oz sultanas
3 tbsps mustard seeds
1 tbsp ground allspice
1 tbsp salt
600 ml/1 pint vinegar
500 g/1 lb sugar

> ***Colourings added to chutney vary according to the type, a dark chutney such as this may contain colouring E150 whereas a lighter coloured one may have E102 in it. Chutney may also contain the preservative E220.***

PICKLED · BEETROOT

Prepare the spiced vinegar: pour the vinegar into an enamelled or stainless steel saucepan. Scald a small piece of muslin or cheesecloth (about 15 cm/6 inches square) in boiling water, wring it dry and put the spices in the centre. Tie the 4 corners together to make a bag; add to the pan with the salt.

Cover the pan tightly and heat the vinegar gently to simmering point, then pour into a bowl. Cover with a plate and leave the vinegar to stand for 2-3 hours.

Meanwhile, heat the oven to 180C/350F/Gas 4. Wrap the beetroot in foil, place in a roasting tin and bake in the oven for 1½-2 hours until tender. Leave to cool, then rub off the cooked beetroot skins. Lower the oven temperature to 110C/225F/Gas ¼.

Wash and rinse the jars. Drain and dry them in the oven. Cut the beetroot into thin slices or small dice and pack into the jars to within 2.5 cm/1 inch of the tops. Discard the bag of spices from the cold spiced vinegar, then pour the vinegar into the jars to come 1 cm/½ inch above the level of the beetroot. Seal the jars, label and store in a cool, dry place.

Makes about 1.4 kg/3 lb

Note: Do not use brass, copper or iron containers for pickling as the vinegar will react with the metal. Use plastic-lined lids or plastic lids as they are acid-resistant.

8 beetroots

For the spiced vinegar:
1 L/2 pints vinegar
15 g/½ oz black peppercorns
1 tsp whole allspice
2-3 pieces whole mace
2.5 cm/1 inch piece cinnamon stick
15 g/½ oz mustard seeds
4 whole cloves
25 g/1 oz salt

Supermarket pickled beetroot may contain artificial sweetener saccharin; colouring E122; and preservative E202. For this recipe a malt vinegar with an acetic acid content of at least 5 per cent will give the best flavour.

acute: problems arising shortly after eating something

a.k.a: also known as

allergen: substance which causes allergic reaction

allergy: acute problems which scientists can explain

anti-oxidant synergist: substance which enhances the effect of the anti-oxidant

carcinogen: chemical which can cause or contribute to cancer

chronic: problems arising slowly after eating something repeatedly

humectant: substance which prevents food from drying out

intolerance: acute problems which scientists cannot explain

mutagen: chemical which can cause genetic damage to living cells

sequestrant: substance which binds trace metals and helps to slow down oxidation

teratogen: chemical which may be responsible for reproductive hazards

E100: Curcumin, turmeric
Type: orange-yellow colouring.
Foods added to: some salad dressings, sausage casings, curry powder, pastries, confectionery, soups.
Health hazards: generally presumed to be safe but not fully investigated.

E101: Riboflavin, or lactoflavin, or Vitamin B2
Type: natural yellow colouring.
Foods added to: used in some processed cheeses.
Health hazards: none known, presumed to be safe.

E102: Tartrazine
Type: a bright-yellow coal tar dye.
Foods added to: one of the most widely used, and easily recognised, additives. Used in many soft drinks, sweets, pastries, coatings, ice-lollies, etc.
Health hazards: generally recognised to be responsible for a wide range of allergic and intolerant symptoms including child hyperactivity, asthma, migraine, and skin rashes; and may cause chronic ill-health, too.

E104: Quinoline yellow
Type: yellow coal tar dye.
Foods added to: used in some edible ices and smoked fish.
Health hazards: there is direct evidence that it provokes intolerant symptoms in some people.

E107: Yellow 2G
Type: yellow colouring extracted from coal tar, a chemical very similar to tartrazine (See E102).
Foods added to: used in some soft drinks, confectionery, cakes and biscuits.
Health hazards: may provoke symptoms of intolerance in asthmatics and those sensitive to aspirin. Has not been tested carefully enough for us to know if it is safe over the long term, but there is some evidence that it is toxic to mice and rats when fed at high doses for long periods.

E110: Sunset yellow FCF
Type: orange-yellow coal tar dye.
Foods added to: confectionery, soft drinks, dessert powders, cereals, bakery goods, snack foods and sauces.
Health hazards: some evidence that it might provoke unpleasant acute symptoms; its chronic toxicity has not been fully studied in animals.

E120: Cochineal, a.k.a. carminic acid
Type: naturally occurring red colouring, but can also be made synthetically.
Foods added to: rarely used, but may be found in yoghurt and sausage casings.
Health hazards: poorly studied, and there is considerable uncertainty about its toxicity.

E122: Azorubine, a.k.a. carmoisine
Type: red coal tar dye, not known to occur in nature.
Foods added to: in some sauces, desserts, soft drinks, jams and packet soup mixes.
Health hazards: not recommended for those suffering from asthma, or sensitive to aspirin. Chronic toxicity has not been properly studied in animals.

E123: Amaranth
Type: red coal tar dye.
Foods added to: soft drinks, sweets, and products imitating cherries, strawberries or blackcurrants.
Health hazards: banned in the USA, USSR, Norway, Sweden and Austria, but permitted and widely used in Britain, despite evidence that it can cause both acute and chronic ill health, including intolerance, cancer and birth defects.

E124: Ponceau 4R, a.k.a. cochineal Red R
Type: red coal tar dye.
Foods added to: some tomato soups, strawberry jam, edible ices and packet mixes.
Health hazards: appears to cause acute problems for asthmatics and those sensitive to aspirin.

E127: Erythrosine
Type: red coal tar dye.
Foods added to: some canned fruits, flavoured yoghurts, cherry pie mixes and fried snack foods.
Health hazards: there is evidence that it provokes hyperactivity and other symptoms of acute toxicity, as well as chronic toxicity to some laboratory animals. The subject of much international debate and controversy. We cannot be certain that it is safe, and it is not worth the risk.

128: Red 2G
Type: red coal tar dye.
Foods added to: some meat products including sausages.
Health hazards: not properly investigated, and so we cannot assume that it is safe.

E131: Patent Blue V
Type: blue-violet coal tar dye.
Foods added to: Scotch eggs.
Health hazards: May cause allergic symptoms in some people. Not fully studied with animals, and not permitted in USA, Canada and Japan.

E132: Indigo Carmine, a.k.a. Indigotine
Type: dark-blue coal tar dye.
Foods added to: some confections, biscuits, dessert powders and gravy mixes.
Health hazards: considered to be safe by some experts, but suspected of provoking acute symptoms by others. Some modest toxicity to laboratory animals, but only at very high doses.

133: Brilliant Blue FCF
Type: blue coal tar dye, yielding a green when mixed with tartrazine (E102).
Foods added to: some canned peas.
Health hazards: may provoke intolerance symptoms especially urticaria (nettle rash), and has contributed to cancer in laboratory animal tests.

E140: Chlorophyll
Type: naturally occurring green colouring, found in grass.
Foods added to: fats and oils.
Health hazards: generally presumed to be safe.

E141: Chlorophyllins, a.k.a. copper complexes of chlorophyll
Type: green colouring produced by a chemical reaction between copper and chlorophyll, which is often synthetically produced.
Foods added to: some preserved green vegetables.
Health hazards: generally presumed to be safe.

E142: Green S, a.k.a. lissamine green
Type: green coal tar dye.
Foods added to: some canned peas, soups and lime drinks.
Health hazards: suspected of provoking intolerant symptoms including asthma and child hyperactivity.

E150: Caramels
Type: brown colourings, with distinctive flavours, made from sugars.
Foods added to: widely used, especially in cola drinks and whisky, but also in malt vinegar, pickles, cakes and biscuits.
Health hazards: their toxicity is complex, poorly researched and barely understood. Some caramels disagree with some laboratory animals.

E151: Black PN, a.k.a. Brilliant Black BN
Type: black coal tar dye.
Foods added to: products containing or resembling blackcurrants, as well as cheesecake mixes and brown sauces.
Health hazards: suspected of causing allergic reactions. Toxic to some laboratory animals at some high doses. Chronic toxicity is not adequately studied.

E153: Carbon Black, a.k.a. vegetable carbon
Type: black colouring made from vegetable matter.
Foods added to: some chocolate cake mixes, concentrated fruit juices and jellies.
Health hazards: suspected of being a skin irritant, and banned in the USA because it is suspected of causing cancer.

154: Brown FK, a.k.a. Brown for Kippers
Type: brown colour, a mixture of six chemicals.
Foods added to: fish, canned soups, chocolate confectionery, dessert and dry mixes.
Health hazards: poorly identified and studied, but suspected of provoking hyperactivity. Animal experiments suggest it may be chronically toxic, too.

155: Brown HT, a.k.a. Chocolate Brown HT
Type: brown coal tar dye.
Foods added to: some chocolate, and especially imitation chocolate products.
Health hazards: scientists do not even know exactly what this is, let alone what it does. It is suspected of provoking some allergic symptoms, and appears to be toxic to some laboratory animals. Not permitted in most European countries.

E160(a): Alpha- Beta- and Gamma-Carotene
Type: yellow colouring, occurring naturally in plant pigments.
Foods added to: some edible fats and oils, margerine, cheese products, cakes and biscuits.
Health hazards: generally presumed to be safe, except when consumed in massive doses.

E160(b): Annatto, a.k.a. annatto extracts
Type: yellow colouring derived from the seed pulp of the annatto tree.
Foods added to: Some cheese products, creamed rice and pastry.
Health hazards: a slight suspicion that it might cause intolerance in a few people, but is generally regarded as safe.

E160(c): Capsanthin
Type: orange colour derived from paprika.
Foods added to: some cheeses.
Health hazards: none known, presumed to be safe.

E160(d): Lycopene
Type: red colouring contained in tomato extracts.
Foods added to: none reported.
Health hazards: none known, presumed to be safe.

E160(e): Beta-8-apo-carotenal
Type: orange-yellowish colouring found in the pulp and skin of citrus fruits.
Foods added to: some packet dessert mixes.
Health hazards: none known, presumed to be safe.

E160(f): Ethyl ester of Capsanthin
Type: yellow colouring derived from plants.
Foods added to: none reported.
Health hazards: none known, presumed to be safe.

E161: Xanthophylls
Type: yellow colouring derived from green leaves.
Foods added to: added to some chicken feeds to colour the yolks of eggs.
Health hazards: none known, presumed to be safe.

E161(a): Flavoxanthin
Type: yellow colouring derived from green leaves.
Foods added to: none reported.
Health hazards: none known, presumed to be safe.

E161(b): Lutein, a.k.a. vegetable lutein
Type: reddish-yellow colouring.
Foods added to: none reported.
Health hazards: none known, presumed to be safe.

E161(c): Cryptoxanthin
Type: yellow colouring derived from corn and marigolds.
Foods added to: none reported.
Health hazards: none known, presumed to be safe.

E161(d): Rubixanthin
Type: yellow colouring derived from carotene and occurring naturally in rosehips.
Foods added to: none reported.
Health hazards: none known, presumed to be safe.

E161(e): Violoxanthin
Type: natural orange-red colouring derived from yellow pansies and some orange peel.
Foods added to: none reported.
Health hazards: none known, presumed to be safe.

E161(f): Rhodoxanthin
Type: yellow colouring isolated from yew tree seeds.
Foods added to: none reported.
Health hazards: none known, presumed to be safe.

E161(g): Canthaxanthin
Type: orange colouring present in mushrooms, the plumage and organs of flamingoes and roscato spoonbills.
Foods added to: biscuits.
Health hazards: none known, presumed to be safe.

E162: Beetroot colour, a.k.a. betanin
Type: reddish-purple colouring found in beetroots.
Foods added to: some oxtail soups.
Health hazards: none known, presumed to be safe.

E163: Anthocyanins
Type: intensely coloured water-soluble pigments which give flowers their colours.
Foods added to: some wines and cranberry juice cocktails.
Health hazards: none known, presumed to be safe.

E163(a): Cyanidin
Type: red colouring derived from plants.
Foods added to: none reported.
Health hazards: none known, presumed to be safe.

E163(b): Delphinidin
Type: blue colouring derived from plants.
Foods added to: none reported.
Health hazards: banned in the USA and Sweden, because considered toxic.

E163(c): Malvidin
Type: purple colouring derived from plants.
Foods added to: none reported.
Health hazards: none known, presumed to be safe.

E163(d): Pelargonidin
Type: brown colouring derived from plants.
Foods added to: none reported.
Health hazards: none known, presumed to be safe.

E163(e): Peonidin
Type: red colouring derived from plants.
Foods added to: none reported.
Health hazards: none known, presumed to be safe.

E163(f): Petunidin
Type: red colouring derived from plants.
Foods added to: none reported.
Health hazards: none known, presumed to be safe.

E170: Calcium carbonate, a.k.a. chalk
Type: white colouring which occurs naturally.
Foods added to: some white flour, bakery products, evaporated milk, sweetened condensed milk and confections.
Health hazards: generally presumed to be safe; very high doses can cause constipation.

E171: Titanium oxide
Type: white surface colourant from a naturally occurring mineral.
Foods added to: some confectionery products and cottage cheese.
Health hazards: generally presumed safe, except when inhaled in large doses when it may be found to irritate the lungs.

E172: Iron oxides and hydroxides
Type: yellow to black colourings. Some organic compounds are used as mixtures.
Foods added to: some packet mixes and salmon products.
Health hazards: none known, presumed to be safe.

E173: Aluminium
Type: surface colourant occurring naturally in bauxite ore.
Foods added to: some sugar-coated confectionery.
Health hazards: there is a low level controversy about the safety of aluminium.

E174: Silver
Type: surface colouring, occurring naturally.
Foods added to: some sugar-coated confectionery.
Health hazards: it appears to be toxic to some micro-organisms, and is suspected of causing gastro-intestinal irritation and skin pigmentation when used in large quantities.

E175: Gold
Type: surface colourant, occurring naturally, but rarely.
Foods added to: some sugar-coated confectionery.
Health hazards: none known, presumed to be safe.

E180: Pigment rubine, a.k.a. lithol rubine
Type: red coal tar dye.
Foods added to: some cheese rind.
Health hazards: suspected of provoking allergenic symptoms and child hyperactivity.

E200: Sorbic acid
Type: commonly used preservative.
Foods added to: some salads, chocolate syrup, cider, cheesecake, cheese spreads and cakes.
Health hazards: a few people appear to be unable to tolerate it, but it is presumed safe for most people.

E201: Sodium sorbate
Type: preservative.
Foods added to: some baked goods and soft drinks.
Health hazards: none known, presumed to be safe.

E202: Potassium sorbate
Type: preservative.
Foods added to: some chocolate, baked goods, soft drinks, pie fillings and glacé cherries.
Health hazards: generally presumed safe, but some suggestion that in large amounts it could cause skin irritation.

E203: Calcium sorbate
Type: preservative and anti-fungal agent.
Foods added to: some chocolate syrup, salads, cheesecake, pie fillings, baked goods and drinks.
Health hazards: none known, presumed to be safe.

E210: Benzoic acid, but also used as a flavouring in the USA. Occurs naturally in many berries, tea and cherry bark.
Type: preservative.
Foods added to: some fruit juices, salad dressings, soft drinks, and pickles.
Health hazards: often presumed to be safe in the West, despite some evidence that it might provoke child hyperactivity, and be a mild irritant to skin, eyes and mucous membrane, but its use is much restricted in the USSR where it is thought to be chronically toxic.

E211: Sodium benzoate
Type: preservative, occurring naturally in many fruits and vegetables.
Foods added to: some carbonated drinks, fruit juices, bottled sauces and cheesecake mixes.
Health hazards: may adversely affect hyperactive children and provoke symptoms of acute intolerance. It has been seen to cause damage to the young of some laboratory animals at high doses.

E212: Potassium benzoate.
Type: preservative.
Foods added to: none reported.
Health hazards: may adversely affect hyperactive children, asthmatics, those suffering urticaria, or aspirin sensitives.

E213: Calcium benzoate
Type: preservative.
Foods added to: None reported.
Health hazards: may adversely affect hyperactive children, asthmatics and those sensitive to aspirin or with recurrent urticaria; otherwise presumed to be safe.

E214: Ethyl 4-hydroxybenzoate
Type: preservative.
Foods added to: some prepacked beetroot and coffee.
Health hazards: may adversely affect hyperactive children and asthmatics and aspirin sensitives.

E215: Sodium ethyl para-hydroxy benzoate
Type: preservative.
Foods added to: none reported.
Health hazards: may adversely affect hyperactive children, and have adverse effects on asthmatics and aspirin sensitives; but otherwise presumed to be safe.

E216: Propyl 4-hydroxybenzoate
Type: preservative.
Foods added to: soft drinks, fish, pickles and salad cream.
Health hazards: may adversely affect hyperactive children.

E217: Sodium n-propyl p-hydroxy benzoate
Type: preservative.
Foods added to: some pickles, fish products, soft-drinks and coffee essence.
Health hazards: may adversely affect hyperactive children and aspirin sensitives.

E218: Methyl para-hydroxybenzoate
Type: preservative.
Foods added to: some baked goods, soft drinks, beer and soups.
Health hazards: may have adverse effects on hyperactive children, asthmatics and aspirin sensitives; but presumed safe for other people, except at high concentrations.

E219: Sodium methyl hydroxy benzoate
Type: preservative.
Foods added to: some soups, salad cream, beverages, pickles and fish.
Health hazards: may adversely affect hyperactive children, as well as asthmatics and aspirin sensitives; otherwise presumed to be safe.

E220: Sulphur dioxide
Type: most widely used preservative and antioxidant.
Foods added to: beer, fruit, sausagemeat, wines, sauces, soups, flour, vinegar and many others.
Health hazards: suspected mutagen and can enhance the action of a notorious carcinogen. May provoke asthmatic attacks in sensitive individuals and cause allergic or nervous reactions in asthmatics, aspirin sensitives, eczema or ulcer sufferers. Destroys vitamin E.

E221: Sodium sulphite
Type: preservative.
Foods added to: cut fruits, fruit juices, fruit pie mixes, wine and beer.
Health hazards: may be an allergen and irritant to asthmatics, eczema and ulcer sufferers.

E222: Sodium Hydrogen Sulphite
Type: preservative.
Foods added to: wine, ale and beer, fruit juices.
Health hazards: destroys vitamin B1, and in US is banned from food rich in this vitamin. May also be responsible for occasional but severe acute and chronic toxicity.

E223: Sodium Metabisulphite
Type: preservative.
Foods added to: sauces, sausages. May also be in fruit juices, dehydrated vegetables and jams.
Health hazards: may cause occasional allergic skin reactions, diarrhoea, stomach upsets. May be dangerous to asthmatics and irritating to the skin and ulcers.

E224: Potassium metabisulphite
Type: preservative and browning agent.
Foods added to: wine, beer and ale. May also be found in fruit juices and dehydrated vegetables.
Health hazards: can cause gastric distress and diarrhoea. Safety has been suspect for some time in US because it may impair the action of nutrients or introduce toxicants. May be dangerous to asthmatics and irritating to skin and ulcers.

E226: Calcium sulphite
Type: preservative.
Foods added to: cider.
Health hazards: may cause stomach upsets. May be dangerous to asthmatics, cause skin irritation and adversely affect ulcers.

E227: Calcium hydrogen sulphite
Type: firming agent, preservative.
Foods added to: jams, jellies and beer.
Health hazards: may cause stomach upsets. May be dangerous to asthmatics, irritate skin and ulcers.

E230: Diphenyl, a.k.a. biphenyl
Type: preservative.
Foods added to: skins of citrus fruits.
Health hazards: the warning 'with diphenyl, peel unsuitable for consumption' must be stamped on US citrus fruit shipped to some European countries. Suspected carcinogen and irritant to the eyes and nose. May cause nausea and vomiting.

E231: Orthophenylphenol
Type: preservative.
Foods added to: skins of citrus fruits.
Health hazards: suspected mutagen and carcinogen. May cause nausea and irritate eyes and nose.

E232: Sodium orthophenylphenate
Type: preservative.
Foods added to: skins of cherries and citrus fruits.
Health hazards: in some test systems, it can cause destruction of chromosomes and can lead to genetic mutations. May cause nausea, convulsions and vomiting. Also may irritate the eyes and nose.

E233: Thiabendazole
Type: fungicide.
Foods added to: skins of bananas and citrus fruits.
Health hazards: none known, presumed to be safe.

E234: Nisin
Type: preservative.
Foods added to: canned foods, creams and cheeses.
Health hazards: none known, presumed to be safe.

E236: Formic acid, a.k.a. methanoic acid
Type: preservative.
Foods added to: baked goods, beverages, ice cream.
Health hazards: toxicity tests on this additive are incomplete. Not permitted in UK.

E237: Sodium Formate
Type: preservative.
Foods added to: bakery products excluding bread.
Health hazards: at high doses absorption may lead to kidney disorders.

E238: Calcium Formate
Type: preservative.
Foods added to: bakery products, but not bread.
Health hazards: at high doses absorption may lead to kidney disorders.

E239: Hexamine
Type: preservative.
Foods added to: some fish and cheese.
Health hazards: a skin irritant. There is also some evidence that it might be chronically toxic.

E249: Potassium Nitrite
Type: preservative and colour fixative.
Foods added to: bacon, cooked cured ham, sausages, salamis, pâtés, smoked fish.
Health hazards: may be hazardous to infants and asthmatics. There is some indirect evidence that it might contribute in the long term to cancer.

E250: Sodium nitrite
Type: preservative and cosmetic.
Foods added to: ham, bacon and many processed and cooked meat, fish and cheese products.
Health hazards: unsafe for infants and young children especially. May contribute in the long term to cancer.

E251: Sodium nitrate
Type: preservative.
Foods added to: many processed meat, fish and cheese products.
Health hazards: E251 decays into E250, and so poses similar hazards. Unsafe for infants and young children especially. May contribute in the long term to cancer.

E252: Potassium Nitrate
Type: preservative and colour fixative.
Foods added to: cured meats.
Health hazards: unsafe for infants and young children. May contribute in the long term to cancer.

E260: Acetic acid
Type: preservative, acidifier and colour diluent.
Foods added to: chocolate, chewing gum, pickles, ketchup, processed cheeses, and vinegar.
Health hazards: vapour from it may irritate the bronchi. Concentrated doses can be extremely corrosive and toxic, but no adverse effects are known when ingested in small quantities. Kills bacteria at concentrations above 5 per cent.

E261: Potassium acetate
Type: preservative and buffering agent. Maintains the colours of plant tissues.
Foods added to: none known.
Health hazards: may cause some blood mineral disorders in people with troubled kidneys.

E262: Sodium acetate
Type: preservative.
Foods added to: crisps and some breads.
Health hazards: presumed safe.

E263: Calcium Acetate
Type: preservative, anti-mould agent and buffer.
Foods added to: packet mixes such as cheesecake and jelly.
Health hazards: presumed safe.

E270: Lactic acid, a.k.a. D-L Lactic acid
Type: preservative occurring in sour milk, fruits, tomato juice and some plants.
Foods added to: beer, carbonated fruit beverages, white bread, rolls, confectionery, salad dressing and certain types of prepared meat dishes.
Health hazards: usually, but not invariably, presumed safe.

E280: Propionic acid
Type: anti-mould agent occurring naturally in dairy products, apples and strawberries, tea and wood-pulp liquor.
Foods added to: flour, confectionery, baked foods.
Health hazards: moderate skin irritant, otherwise presumed to be safe.

E281: Sodium Propionate
Type: preservative, anti-mould agent.
Foods added to: puddings and dairy products.
Health hazards: can cause allergenic reactions such as migraine attacks or skin irritation.

E282: Calcium Propionate
Type: preservative, anti-mould agent.
Foods added to: bread, rolls, chocolate products, cakes, frozen pizza, processed cheeses and artificially sweetened fruit jelly.
Health hazards: can cause allergic reactions with gastro-intestinal symptoms similar to gall-bladder attack. May also contribute to migraine headaches; also destroys the enzyme in the body that normally enables assimilation of any calcium.

E283: Potassium propionate
Type: preservative, anti-mould agent.
Foods added to: sweet baked foods.
Health hazards: presumed to be safe.

E290: Carbon dioxide
Type: preservative, carbonating agent and pressure dispersing agent. Product of yeast formation.
Foods added to: gassed creams, fizzy drinks.
Health hazards: may cause increase in alcohol absorption and high blood pressure.

296: Malic acid, a.k.a. 'apple acid'
Type: acidifier, present in all living cells.
Foods added to: wine, frozen vegetables, oxtail soup and crisps.
Health hazards: it is not known if infants can utilize it. May be hazardous in baby foods. May also act as an irritant.

297: Fumaric acid
Type: acidifier, derived from many plants and is essential to vegetable and animal tissue respiration.
Foods added to: dessert powders, confections, beverages, baked goods, cheesecake mix.
Health hazards: may be an irritant for some people but generally presumed safe.

E300: Ascorbic acid, a.k.a. Vitamin C
Type: Preservative and anti-oxidant.
Foods added to: beer, potato flakes, breakfast foods, cut fruits, meats, flour, stock cubes, bread and baked products.
Health hazards: as ingested in foods, is essential and safe. However, taken in very large quantities it may have an irritating effect causing diarrhoea, nausea, flushing of the face, and headache.

E301: Sodium ascorbate
Type: anti-oxidant and colour preservative.
Foods added to: concentrated milk products, cured meats, smoked turkey and frozen vegetables, baby foods and stock cubes.
Health hazards: presumed safe.

E302: Calcium ascorbate
Type: anti-oxidant and colour preservative.
Foods added to: concentrated milk products, cured meat products, Scotch eggs, and baby foods.
Health hazards: presumed safe.

E304: 6-0-Palmitoyl L-ascorbic acid, a.k.a. ascorbyl palmitate
Type: anti-oxidant and colour preservative.
Foods added to: sausage and cured meats and some chicken stock cubes.
Health hazards: it has been shown to cause toxic effects in rats at high doses but most scientists do not consider these effects relevant to humans. No other adverse effects known.

E306: Tocopherols, a.k.a. vitamin E
Type: anti-oxidant derived from soya bean oil, wheatgerm and green leaves.
Foods added to: found in fats and oils.
Health hazards: is essential and presumed safe.

E307: Alpha tocopherol, a.k.a. vitamin E
Type: vitamin and anti-oxidant.
Foods added to: white flour, enriched white bread and enriched white rice, and sausages.
Health hazards: essential and safe.

E308: Gamma tocopherol
Type: vitamin and anti-oxidant.
Foods added to: edible oils and some sausages.
Health hazards: biological activity in the body is not well understood but presumed safe.

E309: Delta tocopherol
Type: vitamin and anti-oxidant.
Foods added to: frequently found in sausages.
Health hazards: none known, presumed safe.

E310: Propyl gallate, a.k.a. propyl ester of gallic acid
Type: anti-oxidant.
Foods added to: edible fats and oils, some fried foods, lemon juices, baked goods and desserts.
Health hazards: not permitted in baby foods, and not permitted at all in the USSR. May cause irritations to asthmatics, aspirin sensitives or hyperactive children. Gallates have been shown to cause contact dermatitis in bakers and other workers handling them.

E311: Octyl gallate
Type: anti-oxidant.
Foods added to: edible oils and fats, breakfast cereals.
Health hazards: not permitted in baby foods. May irritate asthmatics and aspirin sensitives. Gallates shown to cause contact dermatitis in bakers and other workers handling them.

E312: Dodecyl gallate
Type: anti-oxidant.
Foods added to: edible oils and fats, breakfast cereals.
Health hazards: not permitted in baby foods. Shown cause contact dermatitis in bakers and other workers handling them.

E320: Butylated hydroxyanisole, a.k.a. BHA
Type: anti-oxidant.
Foods added to: very widely used, especially in fats.
Health hazards: there is a great deal of indirect evidence that BHA may be causing both acute and chronic problems, from hyperactivity to cancer.

E321: Butylated hydroxytoluene, a.k.a. BHT
Type: anti-oxidant.
Foods added to: widely used, often with E320.
Health hazards: there is a great deal of indirect evidence that BHT may be causing both acute and chronic problems, from hyperactivity to cancer.

E322: Lecithins
Type: anti-oxidant and emulsifier. Occurring in egg yolk and soya beans.
Foods added to: chocolate, milk powder, margarine, breakfast cereal, bread, rolls, cakes and biscuits.
Health hazards: none known, presumed safe.

E325: Sodium lactate
Type: anti-oxidant synergist.
Foods added to: confectionery.
Health hazards: none known, presumed to be safe.

E326: Potassium lactate
Type: anti-oxidant synergist, acid regulator.
Foods added to: confectionery.
Health hazards: none known, presumed to be safe.

E327: Calcium lactate
Type: buffer and yeast food.
Foods added to: baking powder and confectionery.
Health hazards: none known, presumed to be safe.

E330: Citric acid
Type: anti-oxidant and acidifier.
Foods added to: dairy and baked products, jams, jellies, pickles, carbonated beverages and sauces.
Health hazards: none known, except may cause tooth erosion if ingested frequently or in large doses.

E331: Sodium citrates
Type: buffering agents and emulsifiers.
Foods added to: confectionery, wines, cheese products, ice cream, fruit jellies, frozen fruit drinks.
Health hazards: can alter the urinary excretion of other drugs, thus making those drugs more or less toxic. Otherwise presumed to be safe.

E332: Potassium citrates
Type: buffering agents.
Foods added to: confections, some jellies.
Health hazards: none known, presumed to be safe.

E333: Calcium citrates
Type: buffering agents.
Foods added to: confections, jellies and jams, carbonated drinks, wines and cheese products.
Health hazards: may interfere with results of laboratory tests, including tests for pancreatic function, and abnormal liver function. No adverse effects known, presumed to be safe.

E334: Tartaric acid
Type: anti-oxidant synergist and acidifier.
Foods added to: baking powder, dried white of eggs, wine and sweets.
Health hazards: may be irritating in concentrated solutions, but presumed safe as a food additive.

E335: Sodium tartrates
Type: anti-oxidant and acidifier.
Foods added to: jellies, confections, soft drinks.
Health hazards: tests on patients given therapeutic daily doses as a laxative reveal side effects of vomiting, nausea and abdominal cramps.

E336: Potassium tartrates, a.k.a. cream of tartar
Type: anti-oxidant synergist and acidifier.
Foods added to: baking powder, jams, jellies and soft drinks.
Health hazards: may cause difficulties to people with faulty liver or kidneys.

E337: Potassium sodium tartrate, a.k.a. Rochelle salt
Type: anti-oxidant synergist and buffer.
Foods added to: confections, fruit jelly, jams, cheese, and may also be found in saccharin. Sometimes used in meat products.
Health hazards: none known, presumed to be safe.

E338: Orthophosphoric acid
Type: anti-oxidant synergist and acidifier.
Foods added to: animal and vegetable fats, soft drinks, beverages, cheese products, evaporated milk and cake mixes, meats and sausages.
Health hazards: in concentrated solutions can irritate the skin. May also cause tooth erosion.

E339: Sodium hydrogen orthophosphates
Type: buffering agent and sequestrant.
Foods added to: canned hams, pork shoulders, pork loins, bacon, fizzy drinks, pudding mixes, cheese products and sausages.
Health hazards: known to cause kidney calcification in animals at high doses, otherwise presumed safe.

E340: Potassium hydrogen orthophosphates
Type: buffering agent and sequestrant.
Foods added to: champagne, sparkling wine, coffee whitening products.
Health hazards: none known, presumed to be safe.

E341(a): Acid calcium phosphate (ACP)
Type: buffer and yeast food.
Foods added to: may be found in baking powder, potato snacks, bread, rolls, canned tomatoes, canned sweet peppers, and jelly ingredients.
Health hazards: may cause gastric irritation.

E341(b): Calcium hydrogen orthophosphate
Type: yeast food and dough conditions.
Foods added to: pastry mix, baking powder, cereals, bread, buns, rolls and pie filling.
Health hazards: none known, presumed to be safe.

E341(c): Tricalcium phosphate
Type: anti-caking agent and buffer.
Foods added to: table salt, powdered sugar, puddings, meat, cereal flours, cake mixes.
Health hazards: may cause gastric irritation but generally presumed safe.

350: Sodium hydrogen malate
Type: buffer and humectant.
Foods added to: none reported.
Health hazards: presumed to be safe.

351: Potassium malate
Type: buffering agent and seasoning agent.
Foods added to: none reported.
Health hazards: presumed to be safe.

352: Calcium malates
Type: buffering agent and seasoning agent.
Foods added to: none reported.
Health hazards: presumed to be safe.

353: Metatartaric acid
Type: anti-oxidant synergist and sequestrant.
Foods added to: wine.
Health hazards: presumed to be safe.

355: Adipic acid
Type: buffer, occurring naturally in beets.
Foods added to: beverages, gelatine desserts, confections and baking powder.
Health hazards: none known, presumed to be safe.

363: Succinic acid
Type: buffer and acid.
Foods added to: baked goods and breakfast cereals.
Health hazards: none known, presumed to be safe.

370: 1-4-heptonolactone
Type: sequestrant and acid.
Foods added to: ice cream, baked goods, gelatine desserts and chewing gum.
Health hazards: none known and it is presumed to be safe.

375: Nicotinic acid, a.k.a. niacin or nicotinamide
Type: vitamin supplement and colour preservative.
Foods added to: breakfast cereals, peanut butter, enriched flours, bread, rolls and cornmeal.
Health hazards: safe when used as a food additive as the amount used is small.

380: Triammonium citrate
Type: buffering agent.
Foods added to: none reported.
Health hazards: on interaction with other food chemicals it may lead to a release of ammonia, otherwise generally considered safe.

381: Ammonium ferric citrate
Type: dietary iron supplement.
Foods added to: flour and milk formulae for infants.
Health hazards: none known, and it is presumed to be safe.

385: Calcium disodium EDTA
Type: anti-oxidant synergist, sequestrant and preservative.
Foods added to: French salad dressing, mayonnaise, cooked canned mushrooms, soft drinks and alcoholic beverages.
Health hazards: when fed to young rats in tests, it induced liver lesions, kidney disorder, plus degenerative lesions in the kidney renal tubes. If ingested in large quantities, it can lead to mineral imbalance. It has a therapeutic use in medicine, but side-effects caused indicate that it has the capacity to damage the human kidney.

400: Alginic acid
Type: thickening agent and stabilizer obtained from seaweeds.
Foods added to: ice cream, cheese products, custard, salad dressing and beverages and instant desserts.
Health hazards: none known, presumed to be safe.

E401: Sodium alginate
Type: thickening agent and stabilizer.
Foods added to: beverages, ice cream, custard, instant desserts, baked goods, confectionery, cheese products and salad dressings.
Health hazards: none known, presumed to be safe.

E402: Potassium alginate
Type: thickening agent and stabilizer.
Foods added to: beverages, ice cream, custard, instant desserts, baked goods, confectionery, cheese products and salad dressings.
Health hazards: none known, presumed to be safe.

E403: Ammonium alginate
Type: thickening agent and stabilizer.
Foods added to: beverages, ice cream, custard, instant desserts, baked goods, confectionery, cheese products and salad dressings.
Health hazards: none known, presumed to be safe.

E404: Calcium alginate
Type: thickening agent, and stabilizer.
Foods added to: beverages, ice cream, custard, instant desserts, baked goods, confectionery, cheese products and salad dressings.
Health hazards: none known, presumed to be safe.

E405: Propane-1, 2-diol alginate
Type: thickening agent, emulsifier and defoaming agent.
Foods added to: beverages, ice cream, custard, instant desserts, baked goods, confectionery, cheese products and salad dressings.
Health hazards: none known, presumed to be safe.

E406: Agar
Type: thickening agent and stabilizer extracted from seaweed.
Foods added to: beverages, ice cream, meat glazes, jelly surrounding canned ham, sweetened jellies and frozen custard.
Health hazards: can cause allergic reactions and intestinal disorders, but otherwise considered safe.

E407: Carrageenan, a.k.a. Irish moss
Type: thickening, gelling and stabilizing agent naturally occurring as a gum present in red seaweed.
Foods added to: ice cream, gassed cream, confections, chocolate milk, cheese products, chocolate products, custard, jams and jellies.
Health hazards: suspected carcinogen, teratogen and ulcer inducer.

E410: Locust bean gum, a.k.a. carob gum
Type: thickening agent and stabilizer from carob tree seed.
Foods added to: butterscotch, caramel, chocolate, wine, root beer, ice cream, soups, non-caffeine-containing substitute for cocoa and chocolate, confectionery and baked products.
Health hazards: some patients given additive over 2-year period as a laxative in large doses exhibited some allergic reactions, otherwise regarded as safe when used as a food additive.

E412: Guar gum, a.k.a. jaguar gum or guar flour
Type: thickening agent and stabilizer. A naturally occurring seed gum of plants cultivated in India.
Foods added to: fruit drinks, ice cream, ices, baked goods, bottled sauces, salad dressings, soups, toppings, syrups and frozen desserts.
Health hazards: may cause digestive upsets such as nausea or flatulence if ingested in considerable quantity, otherwise regarded as safe.

E413: Tragacanth, a.k.a. gum tragacanth or gum dragon
Type: thickening agent, stabilizer and emulsifier.
Foods added to: fruit jelly, salad dressing, confections, fruit sherbets, sauces and some cheeses.
Health hazards: rarely a powerful allergen, otherwise regarded as safe.

E414: Gum arabaic, a.k.a. gum acacia.
Type: thickening agent and stabilizer.
Foods added to: jellies, chewing gum, soft drinks, glazes, sugar confectionery and cake mixes.
Health hazards: occasionally can cause allergic reactions such as skin rashes but oral toxicity is low. May be a special problem to asthmatics.

E415: Xanthan Gum, a.k.a. corn sugar gum
Type: thickening agent and stabilizer.
Foods added to: dairy products, salad dressings, ice cream and bottled sauces and toppings.
Health hazards: none known, presumed to be safe.

416: Karaya gum, sterculia gum
Type: thickening agent and stabilizer.
Foods added to: ice cream, baked goods, meats, toppings, sauces and pickles.
Health hazards: animal tests have produced ulceration with large doses in some cases.

E420(i): Sorbitol
Type: sweetening agent, humectant and sequestrant.
Foods added to: confectionery, ice cream, desserts, vegetable oils and soft drinks.
Health hazards: if taken in large doses, may cause diarrhoea or gastro-intestinal upsets, but otherwise presumed to be safe.

E420(ii): Sorbitol Syrup
Type: sweetening agent, humectant and sequestrant.
Foods added to: diabetic confectionery, biscuits, cakes and soft drinks, and ice cream.
Health hazards: may cause diarrhoea or stomach upsets in sensitive individuals, but generally presumed to be safe.

E421: Mannitol, manna sugar
Type: sweetening agent and humectant.

Foods added to: used as sweetener in 'sugar-free' products. Also chewing gum, candy, ice cream, confectionery and desserts.
Health hazards: can cause gastro-intestinal disturbances in sensitive individuals, but generally presumed to be safe.

E422: Glycerol
Type: humectant and carrier solvent (substance which provides a base for other additives).
Foods added to: marshmallows, pastilles, edible gums, meat, cheese, beverages, baked goods, gelatine desserts and cake icing.
Health hazards: in concentrated solution can irritate the mucous membrane, and may also contribute to thirst and high blood sugar levels, but presumed to be safe as an additive.

430: Polyoxyethylene (8) stearate
Type: emulsifier.
Foods added to: fruit sherbet, cakes, cake mixes, frozen custard, egg yolks, toppings.
Health hazards: may cause allergic skin reactions or adversely affect the urinal system causing kidney stones. There is a controversy over its safety.

431: Polyoxyethylene (40) stearate
Type: emulsifier.
Foods added to: fruit sherbet, cakes, cake mixes, custard, egg yolks, toppings and bakery foods.
Health hazards: may cause skin allergic reaction or kidney stones, and there is a controversy over its safety.

432: Polyoxyethylene (20) sorbitan monolaurate, a.k.a. polysorbate 20
Type: emulsifier and dispersing agent.
Foods added to: packet cake mix, fruit sherbet, fillings and toppings.
Health hazards: some controversy over its safety.

433: Polyoxyethylene (20) sorbitan mono-oleate, a.k.a. polysorbate 80
Type: emulsifier and dispersing agent.
Foods added to: dietary products, custard, icing, cakes and cake mixes.
Health hazards: appears to cause cancer in animals at high-dose levels.

434: Polyoxyethylene (20) sorbitan monopalmitate, a.k.a. polysorbate 40
Type: emulsifier and dispersing agent.
Foods added to: cakes, cake mixes, custard, fruit sherbet, fillings and toppings.
Health hazards: appears to cause cancer in test animals at high-dose levels.

435: Polyoxyethylene (20) sorbitan monstearate, a.k.a. polysorbate 60
Type: emulsifier and dispersing agent.
Foods added to: shortening, edible oils, whipped vegetable oil toppings, cakes, cake mixes, cake icings or fillings, confectionery, desserts, beverages.
Health hazards: appears to cause both acute and chronic problems to test animals at high doses.

436: Polyoxethylene (20) sorbitan tristearate, a.k.a. polysorbate 65
Type: emulsifier and dispersing agent.
Foods added to: cakes, cake mixes, doughnuts, vegetable oil toppings, fruit sherbet, custard.
Health hazards: appears to cause both acute and chronic problems to test animals at high doses.

E440(a): Pectin
Type: gelling and thickening agent; occurs naturally in roots, fruits and stems of plants.
Foods added to: beverages, syrups, ice cream, confections, jams and jellies.
Health hazards: none known, presumed to be safe.

E440(b): Amidated pectin
Type: gelling and thickening agent by chemical treatment of pectin.
Foods added to: jellies and preserves.
Health hazards: none known, presumed to be safe.

E442: Ammonium phosphatides
Type: emulsifier.

Foods added to: chocolate and cocoa products.
Health hazards: none known, presumed to be safe.

E450(a): Sodium phosphates
Type: buffer, emulsifier, stabilizer and sequestrant.
Foods added to: cereals, breakfast foods, frozen poultry and other meat products, bread, sausages, cheese spread and cheese products, cream and condensed milk.
Health hazards: none known, presumed to be safe.

E450(b): Sodium triphosphates
Type: emulsifier and texturizer.
Foods added to: meat products, processed cheeses, cheese spreads, bread and sausages.
Health hazards: may disturb enzyme action during digestion in some sensitive subjects, but otherwise presumed to be safe.

E450(c): Sodium and potassium polyphosphates
Type: emulsifier, texturizer, sequestrant.
Foods added to: bread, sausages, meat products, frozen poultry, cheese spread and various cheese products.
Health hazards: may disturb enzyme action during digestion in some sensitive subjects, but otherwise presumed to be safe.

E460(a): Microcrystalline cellulose
Type: emulsifier, anti-caking and dispersing agent.
Foods added to: low-calorie products and high-fibre bread.
Health hazards: none known, presumed to be safe.

E460(b): Alphacellulose
Type: emulsifier and gelling agent.
Foods added to: high-fibre foods.
Health hazards: none known, presumed to be safe.

E461: Methylcellulose
Type: thickening agent, emulsifier and stabilizer.
Foods added to: slimming foods, food products for diabetics, baked goods, beverages, vinegar and in immitation jelly and jams.
Health hazards: has been shown to cause cancer in some animals at some high doses.

E463: Hydroxypropyl cellulose
Type: emulsifier, thickening agent and stabilizer.
Foods added to: none reported.
Health hazards: none known, presumed to be safe.

E464: Hydroxypropyl methyl cellulose
Type: thickening agent, emulsifier, stabilizer.
Foods added to: none reported.
Health hazards: none known, presumed to be safe.

E465: Ethylmethylcellulose
Type: thickening agent, emulsifier, foaming agent and stabilizer.
Foods added to: vegetable fat whipped topping, fruit cake and bottled sauces.
Health hazards: has been shown to cause cancer in some laboratory animals at high doses.

E466: Carboxymethyl cellulose, a.k.a. CMC
Type: thickening agent.
Foods added to: ice cream, beverages, confections, baked goods, icings, toppings, chocolate milk, gassed cream, cheese spreads and certain cheeses, and may be in cheesecake mix.
Health hazards: may cause cancer in some laboratory animals at high doses.

E470: Sodium, potassium and calcium salts of fatty acids
Type: anti-caking agents.
Foods added to: crisps and potato snacks and cake mixes.
Health hazards: none known, and presumed to be safe.

E471: Glyceryl stearates, a.k.a. mono- and di-glycerides, a.k.a. MDG's
Type: emulsifier and stabilizer.
Foods added to: beverages, ice cream, powdered milk, packet soup, cake, crisps, potato snacks, margarine and baked products.
Health hazards: none known, presumed to be safe.

E472(a): Acetic acid esters of mono- and di-glycerides of fatty acids
Type: emulsifier and stabilizer.
Foods added to: beet sugar, yeast production, cheesecake mix, soups, bread and baked products.
Health hazards: none known, presumed to be safe.

E472(b): Lactic acid esters of mono- and di-glycerides of fatty acids, a.k.a. lactoglycerides
Type: emulsifier and stabilizer.
Foods added to: cheesecake mix, soups, bread and baked products.
Health hazards: none known, presumed to be safe.

E472(c): Citric acid esters of mono- and di-glycerides of fatty acids, a.k.a. citroglycerides
Type: emulsifier and stabilizers.
Foods added to: cheesecake mix, soups, breads and baked products.
Health hazards: none known, presumed to be safe.

E472(e): Mono- and diacetyltartaric acid esters of mono- and di- glycerides of fatty acids
Type: emulsifier and stabilizer.
Foods added to: cheesecake mix, crisps, margarine, soups, bread and baked products.
Health hazards: none known, presumed to be safe.

E473: Sucrose esters of fatty acids
Type: emulsifier and stabilizer.
Foods added to: dessert mixes, crisps, soft margarine and cakes.
Health hazards: none known, presumed to be safe.

E474: Sucroglycerides
Type: emulsifier and stabilizer.
Foods added to: crisps and soft margarine, cakes and pudding mixes.
Health hazards: none known, presumed to be safe.

E475: Polyglycerol esters of fatty acids
Type: emulsifier and stabilizer.
Foods added to: crisps and pudding mixes.
Health hazards: none known, presumed to be safe.

476: Polyglycerol esters of polycondensed fatty acids of castor oil
Type: emulsifier.
Foods added to: dessert mixes.
Health hazards: there is some evidence of chronic toxicity to test animals which is very difficult to interpret, but often presumed to be safe.

E477: Propylene glycol esters of fatty acids, a.k.a. propylene glycol
Type: emulsifier.
Foods added to: confectionery, ice cream, toppings, beverages, meat products.
Health hazards: none known, presumed to be safe.

478: Lactylated fatty acid esters of glycerol and propane-1,2-diol
Type: emulsifier and stabilizer.
Foods added to: cakes and dessert mixes.
Health hazards: none known, presumed to be safe.

E481: Sodium stearoyl-2-lactylate
Type: emulsifier and stabilizer.
Foods added to: crisps, potato snacks, cake icings, shortening and edible fats and oils.
Health hazards: presumed to be safe.

E482: Calcium stearoyl-2-lactylate
Type: emulsifier and stabilizer.
Foods added to: various bakery products, and gravy granules.
Health hazards: some animal tests have provided variable and inconsistent results, so some governments have requested further research on this substance. Cannot be presumed to be safe.

E483: Stearyl tartrate
Type: flour treatment agent.
Foods added to: cakes and packet cake mixes.
Health hazards: none known, presumed to be safe.

491: Sorbitan monostearate
Type: emulsifier.
Foods added to: cakes, cake mixes, whipped vegetable oil toppings, milk and cream substitutes for use in coffee and beverages.
Health hazards: none known, presumed to be safe.

492: Sorbitan tristearate
Type: emulsifier.
Foods added to: packet cake mix.
Health hazards: in some sensitive subjects, it may cause the body to take up more liquid paraffin which might irritate the system, but otherwise presumed to be safe.

493: Sorbitan monolaurate
Type: emulsifier and anti-foaming agent.
Foods added to: packet cake mix.
Health hazards: none known, presumed to be safe.

494: Sorbitan mono-oleate
Type: emulsifier and defoamer.
Foods added to: dietary products, chewing gum and packet cake mix.
Health hazards: none known, presumed to be safe.

495: Sorbitan monopalmitate
Type: emulsifier and dispersing agent.
Foods added to: cake mixes.
Health hazards: none known, presumed to be safe.

500: Sodium carbonate, sodium hydrogen carbonate, a.k.a. bicarbonate of soda, sodium sesquicarbonate
Type: buffer, foaming agent, release agent and raising agent. Occurs naturally as saline residues.
Foods added to: canned custard, bread products, cheesey potato snacks and cream.
Health hazards: large quantities may produce corrosion of gastro-intestinal tract, mineral imbalance, vomiting or diarrhoea; but generally presumed to be safe in realistic additive doses.

501: Potassium carbonate, a.k.a. salt of tartar
Type: buffer and alkali.
Foods added to: confection and cocoa products, and some in custard powders.
Health hazards: in large quantities it is an irritant with caustic action, but presumed to be safe at realistic additive doses.

503: Ammonium carbonate
Type: leavening agent, buffer and neutralizer.
Foods added to: baked goods, confections.
Health hazards: large quantities may irritate the mucous membranes of the stomach or cause mineral imbalance in circulatory system, but presumed to be safe at realistic additive doses.

504: Magnesium carbonate naturally occurring mineral
Type: anti-caking and anti-bleaching agent.
Foods added to: ice cream, soured cream, icing sugar.
Health hazards: large quantities may cause upset of circulatory system, otherwise presumed safe.

507: Hydrochloric acid
Type: acidifier.
Foods added to: food starch, and used in brewing.
Health hazards: concentrated solutions can cause severe burns and skin rashes. Inhalation of the fumes may cause choking and also inflammation of the respiratory tract. Large ingested doses may induce ulcers. Reasonable additive doses assumed to be safe.

508: Potassium chloride
Type: seasoning and gelling agent, also yeast food.
Foods added to: canned red kidney beans, salt substitutes, brewing process and gelling process and dietary supplement.
Health hazards: may cause intestinal ulcers and gastro-intestinal irritation in those especially sensitive. Also, large intakes may adversely affect the functioning of the heart in susceptible individuals.

509: Calcium chloride
Type: firming agent.
Foods added to: red kidney beans, apple pie mix, canned tomatoes and sweetened fruit jelly.
Health hazards: none known, presumed to be safe.

510: Ammonium chloride
Type: dough conditioner and yeast food.
Foods added to: bread, rolls, buns.
Health hazards: may adversely affect people with troubled liver and can also cause nausea and acidosis (too much acid in blood or tissues).

513: Sulphuric acid
Type: acid.
Foods added to: used to regulate acidity in the brewing industry and to modify starch.
Health hazards: poisonous substance if used in concentrated form. If ingested undiluted, it can be fatal. Likely additive usage is presumed to be safe.

514: Sodium sulphate
Type: diluent.
Foods added to: none reported.
Health hazards: has marked impact on sodium levels in the body and this can be dangerous for babies or patients with circulatory problems.

515: Potassium sulphate
Type: salt substitute.
Foods added to: none reported.
Health hazards: large doses can cause gastro-intestinal bleeding, but otherwise it is presumed to be safe.

516: Calcium sulphate, a.k.a. plaster of Paris
Type: firming agent, sequestrant and yeast food.
Foods added to: cereal flours, bread, rolls, buns, cheeses, sweet peppers, canned tomatoes.
Health hazards: none known, presumed to be safe.

518: Magnesium sulphate, a.k.a. Epsom salts
Type: firming agent and dietary supplement.
Foods added to: none reported.
Health hazards: little toxicity but may cause diarrhoea at medicinal doses.

524: Sodium hydroxide, a.k.a. lye
Type: alkali.
Foods added to: edible oils and fats, soured cream, butter, cocoa products and canned peas; also found in jams and crisps.
Health hazards: at high doses may cause vomiting and stomach irritation.

525: Potassium hydroxide, a.k.a. caustic potash
Type: alkali.
Foods added to: cocoa products, jams, crisps and cheese.
Health hazards: at high doses may irritate the throat and stomach and cause vomiting with pain.

526: Calcium hydroxide, a.k.a. slaked lime
Type: firming agent and buffer.
Foods added to: fruit products, cheese, cocoa products, jams and crisps.
Health hazards: none known, presumed to be safe.

527: Ammonium hydroxide
Type: alkali.
Foods added to: baked goods, confections and cocoa products.
Health hazards: in large quantities may be caustic and may affect people with faulty kidneys or liver.

528: Magnesium hydroxide
Type: alkali and colour adjunct.
Foods added to: canned peas, cheese and cocoa products.
Health hazards: none known, presumed to be safe.

529: Calcium oxide, a.k.a. lime
Type: alkali, dough conditioner and yeast food.
Foods added to: dairy products, soured cream, butter, confections and tripe.
Health hazards: in concentrated solutions is very caustic and can severely damage skin and mucous membranes, but at realistic additive doses is presumed to be safe.

530: Magnesium oxide
Type: anti-caking agent.
Foods added to: canned peas and some cocoa products.
Health hazards: none known, presumed to be safe.

535: Sodium ferrocyanide
Type: anti-caking agent.
Foods added to: wines.
Health hazards: inadequately studied in animals and humans, and presumed to be safe as long as we do not absorb them in our intestines.

536: Potassium ferrocyanide
Type: anti-caking agent.
Foods added to: some wines.
Health hazards: none known, presumed to be safe as long as we do not absorb them in our intestines.

540: Calcium phosphates, a.k.a. calcium hydrogen phosphate
Type: yeast food and dough conditioner supplement and mineral.
Foods added to: bread, rolls, cereal flours, cheese and some crisps.
Health hazards: animal tests reveal that at certain doses it can cause calcification (hardening) of soft tissues, but generally presumed to be safe.

541: Sodium aluminium phosphate, a.k.a. salp or kasal
Type: leavening agent or emulsifier.
Foods added to: cheese and self-raising flour.
Health hazards: may adversely raise levels of sodium in the body, especially in babies and those with faulty heart or kidney.

542: Edible bone phosphate
Type: mineral supplement and anti-caking agent.
Foods added to: mineral supplements.
Health hazards: none known, presumed to be safe.

544: Calcium polyphosphates
Type: texturizer, emulsifier, moisture retaining agent and sequestrant.
Foods added to: cheeses and packaged meats.
Health hazards: none known, presumed to be safe.

545: Ammonium polyphosphates
Type: emulsifier.
Foods added to: cheese and packaged meats.
Health hazards: none known, presumed to be safe.

551: Silicon dioxide, a.k.a. silica, derived from sand or rock
Type: anti-caking agent.
Foods added to: shaped crisps.
Health hazards: none known by ingestion and presumed to be safe, but prolonged intensive inhalation of the dust can injure the lungs.

552: Calcium silicate
Type: anti-caking agent, glazing agent and acid regulator.
Foods added to: chewing gum coating, meat pies, salt and confectionery, crisps.
Health hazards: none known, presumed to be safe.

553(a): Magnesium silicate
Type: anti-caking agent.
Foods added to: table salt, vanilla powder, packet noodles and some crisps.
Health hazards: none known, presumed to be safe at additive doses.

553(b): Talc
Type: anti-caking agent.
Foods added to: packet noodles, icing sugar, chewing gum base and vitamin supplement.
Health hazards: prolonged inhalation can cause lung damage. The high incidence of stomach cancer among the Japanese is suspected to be due to a diet high in rice which has been treated with talc. At food additive doses it is usually presumed to be safe.

554: Aluminium sodium silicate
Type: anti-caking agent.
Foods added to: packet noodles.
Health hazards: none known, presumed to be safe.

556: Aluminium calcium silicate
Type: anti-caking agent.
Foods added to: table salt, vanilla powder.
Health hazards: none known, presumed to be safe.

558: Bentonite
Type: anti-caking agent.
Foods added to: wine.
Health hazards: none known, presumed to be safe.

559: Kaolin, a.k.a. aluminium silicate
Type: anti-caking agent, naturally occurring in granite in Cornwall and US.
Foods added to: none reported.
Health hazards: none known, presumed to be safe.

570: Stearic acid
Type: anti-caking agent naturally occurring in some vegetable oils and bark extract.
Foods added to: sweets, chewing gum base, vanilla flavouring for beverages.
Health hazards: suspected allergen to sensitive individuals, but presumed to be otherwise safe.

572: Magnesium stearate
Type: anti-caking agent and emulsifier.
Foods added to: some sweets.
Health hazards: none known, presumed to be safe.

575: Galucono delta-lactone
Type: leavening agent and acidifier.
Foods added to: jelly powders, soft drinks powders, beer and milk and packet cake mixes.
Health hazards: none known, presumed to be safe.

576: Sodium gluconate
Type: sequestrant and yeast food.
Foods added to: confections, apple slices, dietary supplements.
Health hazards: none known, presumed to be safe.

577: Potassium gluconate
Type: yeast food.
Foods added to: none reported.
Health hazards: none known, presumed to be safe.

578: Calcium gluconate
Type: buffer and firming agent.
Foods added to: confections, apple slices.
Health hazards: none known, presumed to be safe.

620: L-glutamic acid
Type: flavour enhancer and salt substitute.
Foods added to: savoury snacks, soup mixes, packet sauces, sausages and pork pies.
Health hazards: in some sensitive individuals it can cause nutritional imbalance, burning, facial and chest pressure and headaches; presumed to be otherwise safe.

621: Monosodium glutamate, a.k.a. MSG
Type: flavour enhancer.
Foods added to: very widely used, especially in packet soups and snacks, and enumerable other products.
Health hazards: provokes intolerant symptoms in sensitive individuals, and suspected of causing brain lesions in laboratory animals. Prohibited in foods for babies and young children.

622: Monopotassium glutamate
Type: flavour enhancer and salt substitute.
Foods added to: foods for people with special dietary needs.
Health hazards: in sensitive individuals it can cause burning, facial pressure, headaches, vomiting, nausea, diaorrhea, abdominal cramps and nutritional imbalance. Only permitted in dietetic foods, prohibited in other foods.

623: Calcium glutamate
Type: flavour enhancer and salt substitutes.
Foods added to: foods for people with special dietary needs.
Health hazards: Only permitted in dietetic foods, prohibited in other foods.

627: Sodium guanylate
Type: flavour enhancer.
Foods added to: crisps, potato snacks, gravy granules, pre-cooked dried rice.
Health hazards: should be avoided by gout sufferers and people taking uric acid-retaining dieuretics. Also prohibited in foods for babies and young children.

631: Sodium 5'-inosinate
Type: flavour enhancer derived from meat.
Foods added to: crisps, potato snacks, dried convenience foods.
Health hazards: should be avoided by gout sufferers. Prohibited in foods for babies and young children.

635: Sodium 5'ribonucleotide
Type: flavour enhancer.
Foods added to: crisps, packet soups and potato products.
Health hazards: prohibited in foods for babies and young children.

636: Maltol
Type: flavouring agent.
Foods added to: bread, cakes, synthetic chocolate, vanilla flavouring for beverages, ice cream and baked goods.
Health hazards: prohibited in foods for babies and young children.

637: Ethyl maltol
Type: flavouring agent.
Foods added to: none reported.
Health hazards: none known, presumed to be safe.

900: Dimethylpolysiloxane
Type: anti-foaming agent.
Foods added to: chewing gum, soft drinks, skimmed milk, jams, syrups, pineapple juice.
Health hazards: animal tests reveal curious effects which are difficult to interpret for humans, but usually assumed to be safe.

904: Shellac
Type: glazing agent.
Foods added to: confectionery and fizzy orange drinks.
Health hazards: at high concentrations may irritate the skin, but presumed to be safe used in small quantities as a food additive.

905: Mineral hydrocarbons
Type: polishing and sealing agent.
Foods added to: coating for fresh fruits, confectionery and cheese rind.
Health hazards: might inhibit absorption of digestive fats and, when used at medicinal concentrations, may cause anal soreness and seepage, but food additive usage uses low concentrations.

907: Refined microcrystalline wax
Type: polishing and firming agent.
Foods added to: chewing gum.
Health hazards: none known, presumed to be safe.

920: L-cysteine hydrochloride
Type: improving agent for flour.
Foods added to: flour and bakery products.
Health hazards: none known, presumed to be safe.

924: Potassium bromate
Type: oxidising agent, improver and bleaching agent.
Foods added to: bread and baked products.
Health hazards: at high concentrations it may destroy vitamin E and cause abdominal distress, but presumed to be safe used in small quantities as a food additive.

925: Chlorine
Type: flour treatment agent.
Foods added to: flour, cakes and puddings.
Health hazards: irritant and destroys vitamin E.

926: Chlorine dioxide
Type: flour treatment agent.
Foods added to: flour, cakes and puddings.
Health hazards: highly irritating and corrosive to both skin and mucous membranes, and also destroys vitamin E.

927: Azodicarbonamide
Type: maturing agent for flour.
Foods added to: flour, bread and various baked products.
Health hazards: none known, presumed to be safe.

INDEX